Natural
Pathways
of
New Jersey

D1568439

Natural Pathways of New Jersey

by
Millard C. Davis

Plexus Publishing, Inc.
Medford, NJ
1997

Published by:
Plexus Publishing, Inc.
143 Old Marlton Pike
Medford, NJ 08055

Printed in the United States of America.

ISBN 0-937548-35-9 (Softbound)

Price: $19.95

Illustrations: Valerie Smith-Pope
Cover Design: Bette Tumasz
*All illustrations were based upon original photographs by Millard C. Davis

Dedication

This book is sent on to my wife, Ginny, and our five children in the hopes and beliefs that they will find, if not these, at least similarly wild places by their own definitions and of their own enjoyments, knowing that they will also try to pass them along to others.

Contents

Foreword

One day our older son Pete averred that natural areas in particular are "time sensitive." And so I did recall that Pulitzer Prize winning nature writer Edwin Way Teale had written a book, *Near Horizons,* about the insects of an old apple orchard, a place that in time was covered by the macadam and buildings of a shopping center. Both the original orchard and the one reverted to nature had shown themselves to be truly "time sensitive."

But I still enjoy his book, even as I walk such places, and write about them. In reading about his old orchard, I join the Teale and the place with its adventures of before, and at the same time I visualize similar sites and events to come in my time. Many of those which I have encountered over recent years are here offered in this book, *Natural Pathways of New Jersey.* They will have changed somewhat, even if now and then almost imperceptibly, but hopefully they will lead you to further adventures of your own. Hopefully you will also take with you something for your imagination. I once thought of it this way:

> All about us nature flourishes. And we as a family enter into it. Also occasionally, and especially during winter, we like to bring it indoors. Thus we both partake of the wild in its place and make a home for it elsewhere. In these ways we make nature our own, physically and in our thinking. The latter has probably been the more significant, particularly because it has allowed us more freedom of choice. Through it, ours has become a covenant with all of the outdoors, and hopefully with its Creator, for we have certainly been given at least an ark. An Ark of the Imagination.

However it works out, many memories of the natural places here presented linger. So it is that I recall the time when I was walking with a naturalist in a wooded ravine of northern Jersey and he mused, "I have heard that rattlesnakes such as we sometimes run into here will bite the first person passing by...or was it the second person?"

When working on the Master Management Plan for the then 38 codified Natural Areas of New Jersey, I began to feel that each such place might well have a certain tone which could be expressed in its own plan. Thus for the

Pinelands perhaps a night experience might be invaluable to catch the feel of the place one is partaking of. So in the middle of July I entered Parvin State Park after dusk, and just in time to meet the Ranger who was directing fire engines in an attempt (successful in the end) to quell several blazes from ill-kept cookouts. For maybe an hour my night was one of being with fire wagons as they wheeled about in the darkness like giant lizards. Later we watched dozens of freshly emerged mayflies jiggling in moonlight over the lake. By morning they might all be dead, living hardly twenty-four hours, an event possibly surprisingly the burden of a romantic essay by Benjamin Franklin.

I left Parvin early the next morning to stand in one place where one can meet the first moment of both sunrise and sunset without moving, namely at Cape May Point. In the first light a gull standing on the beach cast a far reaching shadow. I departed to find along the sands of an eastern park a mist that seemed to roll in off the surf. I could see for only a few hundred yards to north and south but hardly at all inland. It made me think of others, those who might have landed here centuries ago and imagined far reaches of this pale shoreline but have no idea of the reach inland of the westward continent.

Then there was a dirt road that slowly dipped down a hill, meandering through a cool hemlock forest, symbol of the far North Woods, and scooping through mixed oaks and maples, more southerly forested domains, to reach a warm woodsy plain; I felt as though I were taking a trip through a table of contents of long miles of our American land.

Finally, on one rainy autumn morning I stood below a pine tree and watched a great horned owl, perched among small branches at the very tip high above, twitch raindrops off its ear tufts.

All of this can mean a life of searching. In *Natural Pathways* you are given places and routes to get there. But the main routes remain within you. The choice is a bit like that of the spider I once came upon:

> Interruption: the some-point of a pause
> or the risk of a conclusion is here defined.
> The spider argues a case for the perfect
> plumb: a guideline with respect
> to gravity or a will to finish the job
> and leave nothing to provisionality.
> Like a thought left untended, the arachnid,
> faintly self-supported, draws from within
> to continue the line. He might have
> retreated.

Or he might never even have begun. I wish you well with your beginnings, some of which might be from among those offered here.

Introduction

A PHYSIOGRAPHIC OVERVIEW

In 1922 German geographer and major general Karl Haushofer established the Institute of Geopolitics in Munich. It was the last great attempt to erect a science which would organize geographical data into formulas for determining potential for world supremacy among Olympian sovereignties.

We ourselves do not need to be so grandiose. We can, however, see a bigger scale to all the individual bits of natural places we have been looking at in New Jersey. One way is to examine the overall geographical scheme of the state.

New Jersey can conveniently be divided by more or less northeast-southwest diagonals into five physiographic provinces. Sedimentary rocks from the middle of the Paleozoic Era, when the first fish and land life appeared as fossils, show their folds and fractures along the northernmost line of New Jersey, in Warren and Sussex counties, making up the Ridge and Valley Physiographic Province of about 635 square miles. The section actually stretches from the north in Canada down into the southern United States. In New Jersey, and elsewhere, this topography has dominated human culture by offering only a thin, acid, infertile, and rocky soil along the ridges but good bottomland deposits in the valleys. Rather neatly, today a number of the bottomland meadows and our resultant cultivating come from ponds created by beavers.

Going south, lower Warren and Sussex counties and beyond them Passaic, Morris, and Hunterdon counties show their affinities with New England. The uplands which form the Green Mountains of Vermont continue here in New Jersey as the diversely structured Highlands Province of about 900 square miles, where glacially scoured lakes lie among heavy ridges of gneiss and similar very hard rock and slender snaking gorges which have been cut through the more yielding limestones and shales. Late in the evening on cold October days, rivers of white mist sometimes stream down the narrow defiles and hover in drifts over the lakes here, vanishing in billows of wet smoke and vertically rising wraiths soon after dawn.

If the upper forty percent of New Jersey were treated as its head, facing westward, then the heavy jaw on back to the cranial bump would be the Triassic Period lowlands of the Piedmont Physiographic Province, a territory of about 1,500 square miles. Here less resistant stone, which is mostly shale, sandstone, and argillite, offer flatter land which is more amenable to farming and settling. In this area, one fifth of all of New Jersey, live about two thirds of its citizens. New Englanders see it in broken patches of Connecticut and Massachusetts, and it continues down into Pennsylvania and Virginia. The result has been that, over its 1,000 mile band, a population corridor has become almost a single metropolis in New Jersey made up of municipalities from the Hudson River down through New Brunswick, Trenton, and Camden.

Oft-times in the Trenton area I have encountered a rather sudden shift from red shales of the Piedmont to the mixed gravels, sands, silts, and clays of the Inner and Outer Coastal Plain Physiographic Provinces, which make up the remaining two thirds of New Jersey. Historically Cretaceous and Cenozoic in origin, they can be followed easily up the coast to Cape Cod and down around Florida into Mexico. In this state cuestas, which are gently sloping bedrock, form a ridge of hills that can be traced southwesterly from the uplands over the Raritan Bay to the lowlands of the Delaware River; they divide the Inner and Outer Provinces into about 1,075 and 3,400 square miles of land respectively. Water of the Inner Coastal Plain drains generally into the Raritan Bay or the Delaware River; that of the Outer drains into the Atlantic Ocean or the Delaware Bay. The Inner region is older of underlying strata, but both are overlain by sediments which were dropped by retreating glaciers. For fossil hunters, stony particles can provide a rich collection of remnants of ancient history which occurred far to the north. Travelers to Europe, incidentally, may walk a similar cuesta partially encircling Paris, which lies within its curve as though on a dish; from this rim of low hills comes the name *Ile de France*, since the ridge was once thought to be a wave-cut cliff left from a lost island. In New Jersey the cuestas of the Coastal Plain are marked by such prominences as Beacon Hill, Arney's Mount, Mount Holly, and Mount Laurel. Clays of the Inner Plain also help distinguish its sandy soils from those of the outer formation. But if you cannot always feel the difference by pressing them between thumb and forefinger, you can often let the surrounding trees tell the story. The greater part of the Outer Plain is the well-known New Jersey Pine Barrens.

In the pyramid of resources and their use, vegetation stands actually, as well as functionally (as part of the flow of nutrients in nature), upon the soil base. Considering the geologic and geographic diversity of New Jersey, then, one should not be too surprised to find here one of the best overall representations of the total upland forested formation east of the Mississippi River. As much as the crests and vales in the northern part of the state cut up the population into small settlements, so the types of plants able to grow elsewhere fragment our society there, especially in the southern region. In this "summer-green" forest, this eastern deciduous forest formation, with its colorful autumn and spring, nearly leafless winter, a new world suggestively similar to yet vastly more magnificent than the one they had left behind faced the first comers from Europe.

Along the northernmost rim of the Ridge and Valley Province hemlocks and white pines show the cold climate affinities of these rough-lands. It is a world left behind in deep, chilly valleys and on dark north-facing slopes by the glacier. In central New England such forests went down on a broader scale during the height of early cultivation, 1730-1750. White pine did return as farms were abandoned during the westward drives a century later, but soon sawmills denuded the landscape once more. In northern New Jersey the terrible terrain would provide countless refuges against massive farming and timber industries, as well as eventually other corporate developments of a maturing society.

South of this region sugar maples of the same hemlock-hardwood forest types become more prevalent, and they are joined by oaks, tulip trees, hickories, and formerly chestnuts in mixed associations there, the Ridge and Valley, Highlands and Piedmont Provinces and the northeastern part of the Inner Coastal Plain. The oaks in particular tell of warming trends which melted the ice in a period which may have been even more temperate than that of today.

Our small oak woods are all that remain of this massive primeval green belt which extended like a great room from eastern Massachusetts to the northern border of Georgia and which lead Captain John Smith to say in his tract *A Description of New England* in 1616 that the main wood here is oak. Though Smith did recognize that oaks might be found in a wide variety of soils, those trees generally implied crop-worthy ground in the northeast. In New Jersey the largest settlements prospered first of all on the lands of this natural resource, this strong second tier of the pyramid of resources. The idea of resource was beginning to change from one meaning the ability of the land to restore itself to one indicating a commodity.

But in the region below, the remainder of New Jersey, one million acres of oak was joined by, often even dominated by, pine. We know this pine, oak, and sand country as the Pine Barrens or Pinelands.

All of these places have seen change, though the larger land forms have been fairly passive. Life forms evolved as a whole, but some remained essentially static. Cockroaches, for instance, seem not to have changed much over their early ancestors of the Pennsylvanian Period, more than 280 million years ago, a time sometimes referred to as the "Age of Cockroaches." In the seas, horseshoe crabs and sharks similarly "progressed" but little, though some of the latter apparently had a period of existence in fresh waters—a fact deduced from their blood being less salty than that of their successors of today.

Flowering plants had hardly appeared on earth when insects began to turn them against themselves by using chemicals which induced leaves to form lumps called "galls," which the insects then inhabited. Then, too, the preference of many insect pollinators for sweets effectively forced nature to develop not only elegant nectar-yielding structures but timed feeding hours, resulting in more than one species of plant getting the insect's attention on the same day. Also there are "nectar guides" which lead the pollinators in for sweets. And traps: the yellow lady's-slipper of our woodlands has a room in its blossom where the bees and others are fed and windows which invite the guests out, of course over devices which collect and sprinkle on pollen.

The major difference I see is that these are a few of the multitude of success stories and that we are not too sure of how man's story will turn out. So we look upon his ways as vastly different. The sum total, however, is that all of us in nature have a role which is perhaps best exemplified by that of parasites. Namely, the successful parasite is one which keeps its host going long enough for the parasitic species to survive.

Man apparently came to the eastern United States about 11,000 years ago, a few thousand years after the Wisconsin ice age lobes had melted back from the northern counties of New Jersey, having driven perhaps as far south as into Hunterdon, Somerset, and Middlesex counties. By the time Europeans arrived, possibly as many as 10,000 Indians were on hand here. They had developed the practice of burning the forests in spring and fall to encourage game, which likes the shorter bushier growth of fresh openings rather than tall trees, and so enhance their own hunting. They cropped the fields, natural and man-made. They eschewed, as did Europeans in their turn, settling in quantity down in the salt marsh flats, up on the rocky ridges and in the glaciated Highlands, and out across the Pine Barrens. All of nature was their home, limited at best by the shape of a watershed; later this *oikos* (house) would be limited to a farmstead at best, a place in town at worst.

Ironically, those very fires which the Indians set for hunting may well have been a major factor in making the southern part of the State inhospitable for homesteading. Leafy accumulations which might have changed sandy soil there toward a loam were bowled away in the conflagrations. Then, too, larger game disappeared as the oaks failed to withstand the constant burns and the land went over to pitch pine, which cannot only sprout back after a blaze but has small wafer-like seeds which require practically barren ground to take hold on. When the Europeans came, they had an initial success in raising crops, for such loose soil is easy to work. Unfortunately, though, it took only a few years of crops to render the soil practically sterile, so one had to have huge acreages to raise anything at all.

In the northern part of New Jersey, the nature of the soils also kept people apart. Not only did ridges and outcroppings divide them but, as in much of New England, the best soils occurred in isolated pockets. So in both north and south Jersey each family or homestead had to be as self-sufficient as possible and to know precisely its territorial boundaries. Just as in New England, living by such necessities lead to a strong sense of individual rights. In New Jersey, this has been one factor which eventually resulted in a vigorous "home rule" for municipalities. County government here, where we now see much of the new resource management legislation being lodged, has historically run a poor second to the rights of the municipalities. The same has generally been the case in New England as well. So both places began with an agrarian culture of small farms which suggests that way of living in Greece during its *polis* period of about 700 B.C. to 300 B.C., when the ties of the farming community of small individually-owned farms, the major community, to the land became so strong that they dominated political thought and values. These farmers fought better, to retain that which they had built, tree and vine cultures which take years to mature, and they went on to give this idea of independence in land ownership and thought to the Classical Period that followed, the period we tend to know best...but our Western values of egalitarianism and constitutional government actually came from the prior centuries of agrarian strength, the strength of individual determinism. It is one which can be eroded over here today by the loss of small farms to monolithic corporations.

Once people did begin to settle into New Jersey, however, the assault on the land was overwhelming. In 1726 the first census of the colonies showed 32,442 people here. By 1784 more than 149,400 people were estimated to live here and by 1790 over 154,000.

Farming had cleared the woods from most of the arable land in central Jersey by 1778, when statehood was formally declared. Industry took a little longer to develop, but soon iron furnaces appeared in force in the southern section to handle bog iron of the Coastal Plain. Their first step had been taken back in 1674 when the Leonard brothers were invited to come down from Lynn, Massachusetts, to construct an iron works in Tinton Falls. Today hundreds of the ruins of small forges are dotted through the Pine Barrens, reminders of the bog iron ore from Batsto which armed American soldiers of both the Revolutionary War and the War of 1812. The circular hearths of the old charcoal burners, now slowly submerging beneath broomsedge and weeds, remind us also of the forests that once were, of virgin timber which gave way to the runts of the modern era. Fires of 1874 and 1885, which went almost unchecked, subtracted another modicum of resource as about 100,000 acres and then 128,000 acres respectively went up in flames.

Eventually the iron industry moved to the regions of the "mountain ores" of the Highlands. Here the story was repeated. A European traveler here in 1783 even noted that one furnace in Union had so decimated about 20,000 acres of forest in no more than fifteen years that it had left itself no further source of energy for fuel and had closed down.

So critical had wood resources become in this part of America that it was written of the Philadelphia area as early as 1748 that speculation was starting.

Speculation of another kind was also building. Benjamin Franklin and Thomas Jefferson had discovered the political structure of the confederated Iroquois Indians, one which demanded government be done by Council. The two colonists had known only rule by government with a titular head. Now they saw how a "Union" could be effected otherwise, and they felt that if "Savages" could do it successfully, so could they. Thus arrived a government of individual states, with branches and group considerations, with eventual consensus.

Finally, in England as the American Revolution was gaining momentum, William Pitt strode before his Parliament and nailed it down in five words, his opinion as to the ridiculousness of trying to put a lock on America: "You cannot conquer a map."

But in the end the English really did, by eventually becoming part of it. And that is where we are now, finding places in New Jersey to become a part of it all, part of a whole.

Some Necessary References

Boyd, Howard P. 1991. **A Field Guide to the Pine Barrens of New Jersey**. Plexus Publishing, Inc., Medford, New Jersey

Collins, Beryl Robichaud, and Anderson, Karl. 1994. **Plant Communities of New Jersey**. Rutgers University Press, New Brunswick, New Jersey

Robichaud, Beryl, and Buell, Murray F. **Vegetation of New Jersey**. 1973. Rutgers University Press, New Brunswick, New Jersey

Widmer, Kemble. 1964. **The Geology and Geography of New Jersey**. D. Van Nostrand Company, Inc. Princeton, New Jersey

Part 1 - Natural Pathways

Atlantic County

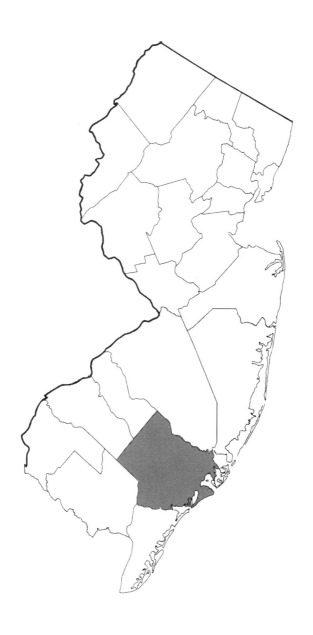

Atlantic County
Absecon

Two natural areas stand out, both just north of Route 30, the White Horse Pike.

The first is a stocked lake and surroundings, known as Heritage Park, in back of the municipal complex. A way to get there from Route 30 is to take Alameda Avenue north, then the second left, on New Jersey Avenue, and then the second right, on Mill Road. This will pass the municipal complex, to your left, so park in the large lot there. A path will take you around the 15 acre lake. Here in a Green Acres supported land the township administrator has told me he has recently seen canvasbacks, American wigeons, and two ospreys—one of the latter "gets a fish about every six tries, about my own ratio," then flies away with the head of the victim pointing forward. Stock includes bass, bluegill, crappies, and catfish.

From farther east on Route 30 you can also turn left on Shore Road and then right on Faunce Landing. It soon passes along broad Absecon Creek and turns left as Fourth Avenue. At this corner is a boat ramp into the creek, which immediately enters Absecon Bay, and a couple of parking places along the road there. You look out over salt water and a salt meadow where crabs crawl, all near the Forsythe National Wildlife Refuge, Brigantine. The birds come in to see you. It is a quiet and rather homey place.

Atlantic County
Estell Manor
Estell Manor Park

These wooded and stream-margined 1,672 acres are the central location for the environmental, educational, recreational, and open space programs of the Atlantic County services. There is room for not only wooded hiking, birding in a variety of habitats, pursuing spring wildflowers, and wetland studies but boating and canoeing, fishing, biking, softball, volleyball, soccer games and camping. One also finds playground space for the youngest.

One of the easiest ways to get here is by taking Exit 17W off the Atlantic City Expressway on to Route 50 and go southwest toward Mays Landing, about 6 miles away. There you cross Route 40 and continue about 3.5 miles to the Park entrance, on your left.

Individuals and groups can do well even further by signing in for nature tours and other programs at the very attractive Nature Center. People at the Center are also broadly aware, once even directing us to a particular road where Brood Two of the 17-year cicadas was offering a giant concert. From treetop level these insects were making a roar that one Center employee said "sounds like machinery." We found that so and equally like a thunderous waterfall's downpour.

Atlantic County
Forsythe National Wildlife Refuge

For wetlands birding right in the middle of the Atlantic Flyway, visit these more than 20,000 acres where cordgrass-saltgrass tidal marsh, fresh waters, fields, and forests. A diked tour road takes you through extensive ponds. Established in 1939 specifically to protect and manage coastal birds that use the flyway, it is open even during winter when over 150,000 birds have been estimated to be visible. A minor fee is requested. A check list of more than 250 species of birds can be picked up in one of the unmanned buildings beside the parking lot. As you travel southeast down Route 561 in Galloway Township and pass under the Garden State Parkway, which has an entrance and exit here, you will soon come to Creek Road, which branches off to your left. Follow this past its crossing of Route 9, and you will enter the refuge. From here you can park and walk trails or continue on, pay your car fee, and drive the circle of diking.

Aside from the bird calendar events, you might want to come during May and June to see the horseshoe crabs sliding up on each other near shore as they mate and spawn. Along the diking is a small shack which you can enter and then look out on the channel below to see this from overhead and without being seen by the big arthropods.

As summer eases into fall, watch where you drive as you travel the dikes, for diamondback turtles may be digging their craters in which they lay their eggs. Large cecropia moth caterpillars may be defoliating some small elderberry trees beside you, and their populations there can amaze you as you wonder how they have survived with all the birds about. And you are sure to notice goldfinches plucking at thistleheads for the down they will use to line their nests, woven late perhaps in response to nest-usurping cowbirds, which prefer to breed earlier.

For many people the most magnificent times come with the shimmering ribbons of thousands of flocked snow geese gliding in during October and November. Soon the waters and banks suggest fields of cotton.

Atlantic County
Wharton State Forest
Batsto Natural Area

An area of over 150 acres, which includes the Batsto Natural Area and the Great Swamp Nature Area, this New Jersey State designated preserve in the Pine Barrens is on the north side of County Route 542 about five miles west of the juncture with County Route 563 and seven miles east of the juncture with State Route 30 in Hammonton.

Wharton State Forest consists of about 100,000 acres that were bought from the estate of Joseph Wharton in 1954, a magnate in Philadelphia whose name you will recognize from the Wharton School of Business at the University of Pennsylvania. Wharton himself had originally some 80 years before hoped to control the sale of underground water here as a supply to Philadelphia and environs. Unfortunately for this lucrative prospect, the New Jersey state legislature learned of it and squelched the deal.

The name Batsto apparently comes from the Swedish "Batstu," meaning a bathing place. Thus it was that waters of Batsto Village were dammed in 1766, with the resultant water powering two hammer wheels and four bellows. An iron furnace in the village used local bog iron—an iron oxide which is leached from sand in bogs and streams and collects in rotting plants, often easily seen as rustlike fluffs along the banks—to make kitchenware such as stoves and kettles and, during the Revolutionary War, cannons.

The present wooded site, which also has a state Division of Parks and Forestry visitors center as well as the Batsto Village Historic Site and plentiful parking, has been designated by New Jersey as a place to demonstrate plant associations which are typical of southern swamp and floodplain habitats. It contains rare and vanishing species of plants and is associated with an area of cultural and historical interest. You will find walking in the oak woods here easy and pleasant, the Batsto and Mullica Rivers with its Sleeper Branch and the Nescochague Creek meandering and dark with the tea-colored water of cedar trees, the cedar bogs blossoming brightly in spring, all being typical representatives of the Pine Barrens.

Essentially there is something for everyone, for Batsto Lake and a barge canal are near the parking lot while footpaths include about two miles of nature trails and 25 miles of the Batona Trail, running from Evans Bridge to Batsto, Quaker Bridge, and eventually the lookout tower at Apple Pie Hill. If you choose to walk on a spring evening, listen for the rapping sound of calling carpenter frogs. During their nesting seasons birds which you can hear after nightfall will include barred and eastern screech owls, common nighthawks, and whip-poor-wills, the voice of the latter especially warming when coming from up near a roof ridge.

Bergen County

Bergen County
Mahwah Township

Here along the northern border of New Jersey where this state meets New York State, the wildlife sanctuary and public park (picnicking, fishing, and walking) known as the Ramapo Valley County Reservation lies in gently mountainous country along Route 202, Ramapo Valley Road. One way of getting there is simply by taking 202 south off Route 17.

As you enter the 2,000 or so acre Reservation and look up the flat waters of the Ramapo River, you are filled with a sense of peace, which might be a valuable theme for these wooded and open acres. More than eight and one-half miles of trails help you range over this happily varied countryside of river, lake, marsh, swamp, and highlands next to Ramapo College.

Bergen County
Tenafly Borough

At the northeastern corner of this borough, where Hudson Avenue terminates in a wooded parking lot, the 50-acre Tenafly Nature Center offers you an attractive interpretive building, several tree-covered paths, and a cattail marsh, with a short boardwalk. School, weekend, and family programs are a feature of their activities. Also trips to far places, such as New England.

On one October afternoon there, I found the trails carpeted with yellow leaves. Without looking overhead, I could in them see tulip trees, black birches (break off a twig and chew the end for its sweet birch beer taste, which makes the bark a fine brew as a tea), black guns (the leaves later to turn blood red), sweetgums, grapes, and ferns. I thought of Robert Frost's poem of two roads parting in a yellow woods. I was sung to by the trilling of bush crickets filling this woods.

To get there from 9W take East Clinton Avenue, Route 72, eastward to County Road, Route 501, and turn right. Hudson juncture will shortly appear, and you turn right again.

Burlington County

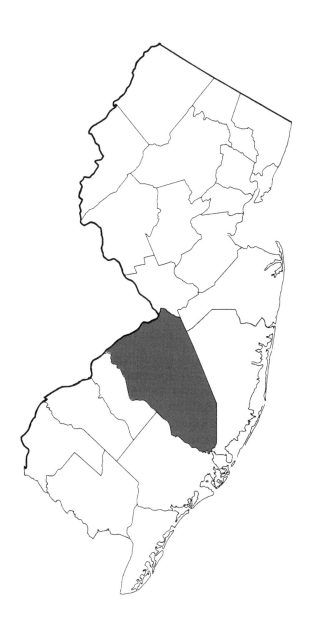

Burlington County
Bordentown Township

Just off Route 206, the small Northern Community Park seems a needed break from the dominating urban nature of this area. You can get there easily by turning off 206 onto Groveville Road just over a mile north of the separation of 206 from Route 130. The park will be on your left within a few hundred feet. Here you will find a mixed approach of tennis courts, baseball fields, pond, picnic tables and benches, and a paved walk around the whole. For birding, get there early, which is just as well for the best viewing anyway. The pond is marshy, so with a net you should be able to show children insect and other life of standing fresh waters.

Farther to the south, as you come up 206 from the New Jersey Turnpike Interchange, go just over one and a half miles and turn right (east) on the Bordentown-Chesterfield Road. Just over a half mile down that a left on Charles will soon bring you to Joseph H. Lawrence Park on your right. Here is another athletic field with partially ringing woods. Nature here is mostly limited to the edge-of-the-woods, but that is a study of its own. The line between lawn and woods is so sharp that you can even take a baby carriage or stroller along this charming interface.

Burlington County
Easthampton

Easthampton is bounded on its eastern side by Route 206, and its southern line runs close to east-west Route 530 (which to the west becomes Route 38). All of this makes access to the Smithville County Park rather simple. Simply take the Smithville-Jacksonville Road immediately west of Rt. 206 north from Route 38 for a little less than a mile and turn left at the indicated entrance. Or go west off Rt. 206 on Powell Road (the first major road north of Rt. 530) and then left on Smithville-Jacksonville Rd.

In the park is a small woods with a deep, steeply banked creek, and you can walk along here on the "Ravine Nature Trail." On the north side of this woods you can look out on some farm fields, so you are effectively at the edge of two habitats. In weeds along the border you may find dozens of the walnut-shaped egg masses of the Chinese mantis and the longish ones of the Carolina mantis.

There is a parking lot right beside the park entrance, and from here it is about a 100 yard walk to the trail and a 20 yard walk to the historic building area where the park office is and from which guided tours emanate.

Another entrance to the property occurs on the north side of West Railroad Avenue, which is your second left if you leave Rt. 530 on the Smithville-Jacksonville Road.

Burlington County
Evesham

Travelling on Route 73 south of the Route 70 crossing, turn east at the light just over 2 miles down and enter Braddock Mill Road. Then go left on Tomlinson Mill Road and left again on Kettle Run Road. Jennings Lake will be on your left. You can park in two small widenings of the shoulder along Kettle Run or try for the mud lot beside the north corner of the lake. Your best finds here will most likely be dragonflies and arrowhead aquatic plants, but it can be a pleasant pause either early in the morning or late of an evening.

If you go out back on Kettle Run and continue with it for about a mile and a half, park at a sharp left curve and walk along the road for a hundred feet or so. You are facing a drying bog on the south side. During wet summers you may find enough orchids and sundews to give you the feeling of more aquatic places, while from early in spring on the voices of frogs will warm you with a wish to stay late.

VSMITH-POPE 95

Burlington County
Moorestown

Largely lying along the north side of Route 38, this attractive township appropriately has set aside four appealing natural areas, and they can be enjoyed by almost anyone.

The most quickly accessible to the outside would most likely be Strawbridge Lake and environs, which begin along the northern shoulder of Route 38 and swing northward in a big lazy right angle. Go north from 38 on Church Road and then quickly make a left turn on Haines Drive, which ends about a mile and a half later on Route 537, King's Highway. You can park along Route 38 under trees or, more popularly, in pulloffs all along Haines. This is a park given over to popular low-level equipment use such as picnicking on blankets, playing catch, watching birds (especially the many Canadian geese and ducks that crowd in here), skating, and so on.

A hidden path through woods along the eastern edge of Strawbridge starts at the end of Nixon Drive, which is off Route 38 just east of the Moorestown Mall. This trail is an extremely attractive half-mile corridor from which you can look out on the lake from hiding as it were. Thus behavioral activities of the birds are easy to watch for long periods of time. Long slender river birches, bulging arrowwoods, and others bow out over the lakeside, and in here under their arch frogs, turtles, insect larvae, birds, and so on shelter close to you. During spring and summer this long room gives you an amphitheater of sound.

If you follow Church Road farther north, turn right on New Albany Road after about 2 1/2 miles. Turn left at its termination at Riverton Road and then left about 3/4 of a mile later on North Riding Drive and finally left on Georgian Drive. At the end of this road, park and walk forward into unmarked Pompeston Creek Park. You will find a spreading lawn with banks of shrubs, and if you go more or less straight ahead you will discover a path into woods. Soon you will be paralleling narrow and shallow Pompeston Creek, and half a mile later cross New Albany and walk another half mile to the end of Bethel Avenue, a good place to turn around and head back. All through here you will be enjoying fair solitude and damp, but not too damp, woodland ecology.

If you take Mount Laurel Road north off Route 38, take your first right, on East Main Street (King's Highway), then right again on South Stanwick. This will bring you into a school parking lot. Park and walk along the border of the woods until you find a path opening. Inside you will find uplands, a ridge, and wetlands...pretty fair variety. During busy times you may be disturbed by automobile and truck sounds from Route 38, which is the southern border.

26

Burlington County
Mount Laurel Township

Laurel Acres Park can be reached by taking Church Street south off Route 38 for about two miles. The entrance will be on your left about three quarters of a mile after you pass under Route 295 and the New Jersey Turnpike.

Here you will find a large open expanse with plenty of parking space, a pond, a hill for sledding, and a wooded edge. Birders may find this area very attractive, especially early on summer mornings.

Spencer Memorial Park can also be reached off Route 38. Just over a mile and a half east of the spot where 38 crosses over the New Jersey Turnpike take Ark Road north; turn right a half mile later at the first crossroad, Marne Highway, and then left a half mile after that on Creek Road and almost immediately after right on Rancocas Boulevard. The park, largely an athletic field surrounded by woods which have some trails, is just over a half mile up on your right. Plenty of parking space is available in season, but during winter driveway access off Rancocas is eliminated by a wire gate.

This park is another situation of wanting to be there early, if going during the summer. Other than that, being easily able to enter the woods makes for a natural charm.

Burlington County
Westampton
Rancocas State Park

Although this wooded park of about 170 acres has a state-preserved Natural Area of about 80 acres, most of it is accessible only by crossing big North Branch River and the Timbuctoo Feeder of the North Branch. Your best moments will be on the property of the Rancocas Nature Center of the New Jersey Audubon Society at that park. Here 30 acres of fields, woods, and wetland together with easy trails and lookout points will give you fine variety. Adjoining are the grounds of the Rankokus Lenape Indian Council; keep alert for the American Indian Arts Festival which is held here every October and brings in Indian artists from as far away as Central America.

Somewhat different for this part of the state are the plantation of tamarack trees and the tidal freshwater marsh, with hollies and wild rice plants, the latter particularly attractive to bobolinks. Also unusual is the long shed where, near eye level, many cliff swallows nest among mudwasp nests, including the remarkable organpipe type of insect architecture. You will also want to come here during summer to walk the trails and perhaps see a glowworm lighting briefly. Then, during mid-autumn, purple leaves of arrowwoods give the lowlands a distinctive tone when the sun is bright and low enough to angle through the woods.

The Nature Center offers a well-written trail guide with 29 stops identified. Two birdfeeders right outside a window bring in a steady crowd of visitors. The bookstore has numerous volumes, chosen well and covering not only New Jersey and North America but a number of foreign places and species as well, in keeping with the long reach of the many travel programs. Naturalists and, of course, a teaching program for schools are also available and are used regularly.

To get to the Center, go east off Route 295 at the 45A Exit, Willingboro being to the west there. You will then be on Rancocas Road. The Center will be about 0.6 miles along, with the entrance to your right—the sign shows up precipitously on a curve, so be ready for its suddenness.

Burlington and Ocean Counties
Lebanon State Forest

Lebanon State Forest is easily driven into from entrances off either of the state Routes 70 or 72, which meet in its northwestern corner, Four Mile Circle. This pinelands tract of about 22,216 acres straddles an apparent divide from which streams go east to the Atlantic Ocean and west to the Delaware River. Small streams wander in the oak-pine woods, but you will find only two ponds. Pakim is colored by cedar water and named from the Lenni-Lenape word for "cranberry," a crop it was used to flood in the nearby bog. It lies near the state office. Deep Hollow, lies just north of Route 70 and east of 72.

The park superintendent's office, near the entrance off Route 72 just south of 70, will tell you how to get to Reeves Bogs, where cranberries are still cultured. If you are interested in seeing a cranberry harvesting operation, which takes place around Columbus Day, also ask at the office.

About six and a half miles farther east on Route 70 from the Four Mile Circle, you will come to Route 530 which goes northwest. It will take you to Whitesbog, 1.2 miles up on the right, an educational and historic site with bogs and blueberry culturing. Original research into blueberries as a potential cash crop took place there, and, more recently, a strong school of nature and conservation education was centered in the buildings.

In the main forest, off Routes 70 and 72, roads and footpaths will take you through many ecological niches with their wide variety of lives. You might come upon a rattlesnake, but they are only occasionals. Years ago, Asa Pittman of Upton Station caught and sold them and so was dubbed "Rattlesnake Ace." The name "Lebanon," by the way, comes from the Lebanon Glass Works which came in during 1862, having found the site excellent for its sand, but left five years later after the wood it used to make charcoal had been diminished.

Birds and butterflies dash or float through the trees with sunlight filtering down past the needles, cicadas whine late in the afternoon, deer slip across your headlights, snow plummets off bowing branches, all of nature combines to make this a sort of paradise in oak and pine land. Here you come for red-headed woodpeckers and the diminutive saw-whet owl. Bobwhites swoosh from brush ahead. You camp so as to live under the throaty shaped song of whip-poor-wills and to walk quietly occasionally on beds of needles as you step carefully around the crackle of old oak leaves.

Camden County

Camden County
Cherry Hill Township

Located along Route 70 at Exit 34 off Route 295, this suburban community has three prominent natural areas, all set aside by the township.

Just off Route 70 several blocks west of 295 is the Barclay Historic Farmstead. Here about 32 acres are given to a brick farmhouse of the early 1800s, garden plots for rent, and a forest, marsh, and pond reserved for wildlife. A trail takes you through woods and around the marsh, which is generally populated by ducks and an occasional great blue heron and kingfisher. Raccoons, opposums, squirrels, and so on walk here. Butterflies jump from flower to flower by day, moths wing in at night. You can get here by taking West Gate Drive south and then bearing left at the fork, continuing down this, Barclay Lane, until a few blocks along you see the farmstead on your left.

The Magic Forest stands as a tribute to beech trees being able to congregate even this far south of their more natural power base, mostly north of the Massachusetts/Connecticut northern line and appropriately westward. Here among tall trees, essentially branchless up to the height of a two-story house, a hawk may beat by overhead as it comes in to its nest. The flooring of leaves is soft underfoot. The calling of insects from the canopy at night suggests voices in a room. A way of getting here is by taking Springdale Road south off Route 70 several blocks east of the 295 exit. Turn right on Kresson Road and then take your fifth left, on Bunker Hill Drive. Soon the sign "Magic Forest" will appear on your right.

Better parking can be had by continuing and turning right on Liberty Bell Drive, then almost immediately right on Bobwhite Drive. At the end of this, on Lark Lane, turn to your right, park, and walk into the woods. Also you can continue driving around first down Lark, then right on Gatewood Road, and finally right on Garwood, where soon a spur to your right offers another parking place where you can enter the woods—really only about a hundred feet from the Lark Lane entrance.

Cherry Hill has set aside a fairly wild 13 acres as its designated Natural Area. A simple way of driving here is to take the Berlin/Gibbsboro Exit off Route 295, namely the first exit south of the Route 70 Exit, and go toward Haddonfield/Voorhees/Gibbsboro, basically south. Now take your first right, Browning Road, and then left about a mile later on Walt Whitman Boulevard. Pull in and park. Then walk out across Burnt Mill and enter the rough thicket land of this fairly untouched plot.

Of greatest interest here is the stream to your right. In a woods, deep of gorge, it winds among trees with their feet in its bed and their canopy up at your eye level. Thus in standing on the bank, after having perhaps fought your way through dense underbrush, you are looking right into the heart of massed tree crowns. Birds singing, mating, nesting, and so on are all directly before you. Paper wasps that hang their gray cities from limbs hum past your head.

And then if you want a woodland pond experience, go left at your entry and down a slope to a dark shallow pond. It struggles for existence here, but so far enough water accumulates each year to entice in a duck or so.

Between these two lowlands lies a flat field that is overgrown by goldenrods, raspberries, shrubs, and the first fighting beginnings of a forest. Thus you have a multiple habitat which in a small arena can offer excellent moments for photographing nature.

Camden County
Haddonfield
Crows Woods

This approximately 30-acre preserve of woods and streams, a place for both social and private bird watching, has a large parking lot at its entrance. On adjacent athletic fields dozens of us have been out nights following astral constellations and even the recent comets. From Route 70 at its juncture with Route 41, you follow the latter, also known as Kings Highway, into Haddonfield for about 2.0 miles. Now turn left, at a light, onto Warwick Road, which you take for 0.8 miles to Upland Way, on your left, and go down it for 0.45 miles to an overpass and the immediately following driveway to Crows Woods, on your right. The Woods are about 0.2 miles ahead and past a playhouse and the athletic fields to your left. The Highspeed Line is to your right and may be rumbling. Warwick Road also, incidentally, meets Route 30 a little farther beyond Upland Way.

Cape May County

Cape May County
Cape May Courthouse
Norbury's Landing

From Route 47 take Bayshore Road, Rt. 603, in a big swing west. Take Atlantic Avenue west off it and drive to the end, where you can park and either walk the beach or sit on a bench for a snack. The overall beach scene here is quite like that at the better known Pierce's Point. This helps spread out the birding crowd during peak seasons, especially significant if you want to do some serious photographing or recording. Bringing your own small chair and a field guide to birds also fits the easy scene.

Cape May County
Cape May Courthouse
Reed's Beach

From Route 47 take Reeds Beach Road, Route 655, west to its end. From the small parking area there you can step up to the bank and observe various shorebirds, including possibly Forster's terns, and also watch Artic terns swinging and diving for fish. You are just far enough away from such activities that you might wish you had a telescope on a tripod.

Cape May County
Cape May Courthouse
Wetlands Institute

From Exit 10B on the Garden State Parkway take Route 657, Stone Harbor Boulevard, east for about 2.5 miles. The Institute will be on your right. Designed for education and research, the building has a large lecture room, with at least one telescope for looking out the bay windows, a fine bookstore, and grounds for walking and watching shorebirds. Be prepared to be assaulted by deer flies in season. Be alert for the many programs offered here.

Cape May County
Cape May State Park
Cape May Point Natural Area

This oceanside 100 or so acres, within a park of about 300 acres, shows typical southern New Jersey sand dune and freshwater marsh habitats, abandoned fields and transitional woods, and it has a nature trail. Designated by the state to be a bird sanctuary, it has been regarded as one of the best birdwatching locations in the United States. In fact the park has been chosen by the New Jersey Audubon Society's Cape May Observatory as a place for its annual hawk watch during autumn when these raptors follow migrating shorebirds and others down the Atlantic Flyway and all of them pile up here before launching out over Delaware Bay and the Atlantic Ocean. The New Jersey Audubon Society also has its autumnal Cape May Weekend here and around. Passing ospreys are also significant during this season.

You can drive here from U.S. Route 9 and the Garden State Parkway by taking Route 109 southward through Cape May City, turning right (west) on Sunset Boulevard (Route 606) and taking it to Route 629, at which point you turn left and drive 0.7 miles to the park entrance; from a point farther west on Route 9 a street crosses the Cape May Canal and also meets Sunset Boulevard, where you will again turn left. The park is easily identifiable by its 170-foot tall lighthouse, constructed in 1859.

About two miles of trails, including a boardwalk and a trail for people in wheelchairs, will introduce you to the park as well as the natural area itself. You will really want to be here during the peak bird migration periods—just as you would benefit from going during the hawk flow to the hawk lookout at Kittatinny Ridge up at High Point in northern New Jersey. You might even enjoy being here, or at least nearby after the park closes, before dawn or after dusk. Listen then to wind in the tall reeds known as phragmites; watch the lighthouse beam swinging around overhead; smell salt water now when your attention can focus on it most clearly. At the Point you can do two other things from the exact same position: watch both sunrise and sunset come in.

Cape May County
Cape May Wetlands Natural Area

This Green Acres funded site shows saltmarsh habitats especially well. It can be reached by crossing the canal via the bridge from Route 9 and taking Sunset Boulevard to the right toward the lighthouse and the bay, then turning left on Lighthouse Avenue. The open land of about 1,750 acres is a sanctuary for typical colonial nesting and migratory birds.

Cape May County
Dennisville
Dennis Creek Wildlife Management Area

Off of Route 47 take Jakes Landing Road south. Standing in the small parking lot near the boat ramp, we saw in the white pine woods nearby a long-billed marsh wren, a male cowbird, and an eastern kingbird one day early in July. Boyle notes that these woods also attract yellow-throated warblers to nest. Various shorebirds and wintering bald eagles are also said to collect here.

Cape May County
Dias Creek
Pierce's Point

From Route 47 take High's Beach Road west to its end. Here from a small parking area you can walk the beach or stand on rocks and view the scene. One day late in summer when horseshoe crabs were laying eggs along the beach, you could hear from a quarter of a mile away the squawking made by the scores of laughing gulls which had come to feed on the eggs. I tried a few of these minute gems and found them to taste peppery.

Cape May County
Stone Harbor Bird Sanctuary

From Exit 10B off the Garden State Parkway take Rt. 657, Stone Harbor Boulevard, past the Wetlands Institute east to its end. Turn right on either Third or Second Avenue and drive south until you see the enclosed woods that are bracketed by Third and Second, 111th to the north and 117 to the south. Off Third you can park and look for birds through pay telescopes; at the end of Second is a parking lot. Here can be a good opportunity to see cattle, great, and snowy egrets, little blue and tricolored herons, black-crowned night-herons, glossy ibis and so on. The flights of nesting birds leave in morning and return in evening and are stunning when seen then from the parking lot.

Cape May County
Strathmere
Corson's Inlet State Park
Strathmere Natural Area

Lying off Ocean Drive between Strathmere and Ocean City to the north, these 80 or so acres of about 341 total acres of general salt marsh and dune environment show dune habitats with special attention to the effects of erosion brought on by tidal movements in conjunction with outwash currents. Also on the western side of Ocean Drive, you will find plenty of saltwater marsh territory and tidal channels. A typical barrier beach lies along the northern side of Corson Inlet, and the south has sand flats (Whale Beach). Egrets, herons, horned larks, snow buntings, double-crested cormorants, laughing gulls (the subject of a recent study in behavioral psychology), black skimmers, piping plovers (watch for their "broken wing" act if during their breeding period you approach their nesting sites on the sand), and many others are here.

From Exit 25 of the Garden State Parkway go east on Route 623 toward Ocean City. In a couple of miles turn right on West Avenue, Route 619, and then right again on 55th Street, Ocean Drive, and look for the sign to park.

Cape May County
Cape May Point
Lily Lake (or Lake Lily)Cape

From Cape May Point State Park go right on Lighthouse Avenue and after about half a mile go left on Lake Drive. Right away pull off and park on the right, where you will see a sign for the Cape May Observatory with Lily Lake across the street. Both the lake and the adjacent woods, where you will find the observatory, are especially excellent for migrant birds. The observatory has a small bookshop and a staff that offers birding fieldtrips and classes.

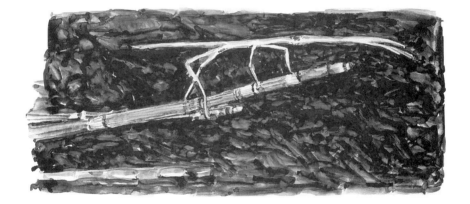

Cumberland County

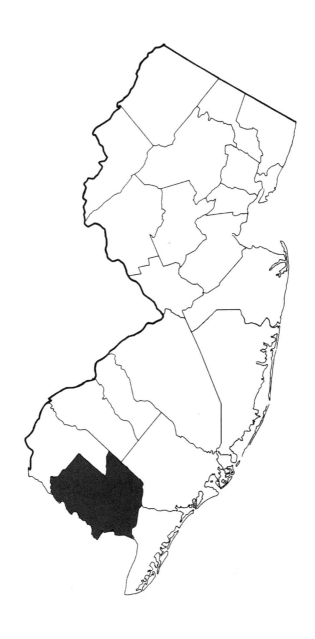

Cumberland County
Commercial Township
Turkey Point Wildlife Management Area

From Route 553 just east of Dividing Creek, turn south on Hansey Creek Road. After woods you will come to an open marsh and boat ramps where there is parking. This area is like the adjoining Egg Island Fish and Wildlife Management Area. Both are especially worth going to at night during mating season for the birds calling.

Cumberland County
Downe Township
Egg Island-Berrytown Wildlife Management Area

Take Route 553 into Dividing Creek and then Maple Avenue south. It becomes Gandy Road and travels through uplands to its end in tidal marsh. In the woods of this 8,325 acres you can find chuck-will's-widows, great horned owls, and whippoorwills, while out in the marsh woodcocks, willets and other shorebirds nest along with black ducks, gadwall, teal, widgeon, shovelers, and others. Keep an eye out for king and Virginia rail during migration seasons. Nesting towers have been set up for peregrine falcons. The tidal creeks are home to crabs and white perch. Out in Delaware Bay you should find weakfish, bluefish, fluke, sea bass, and black drum.

Cumberland County
Maurice River

At the northeast corner of Rt. 49 and Rt. 671, Union Road, the Meadowood Environmental Sanctuary and Recreation Area offers several acres of nature trailing, bird watching along a lake, canoeing, and fishing. It's a very open and relaxed site, so come early to avoid what might be intrusive recreationers. Probably most of the wildlife here will accept both of you, of course.

Cumberland County
Maurice River Township
Corson Fish and Wildlife Management Area

Off Route 47 just south of Rt. 616, Glade Road, go south on Moores Beach Road. On the west side of this road you will see numerous tree stubs ten to twenty feet tall out in the water, excellent perching sites. Beyond this in the soggy meadows, least bitterns have been seen nesting. Moores Beach itself will be worth going to especially during May for the many shorebirds gathering there.

Cumberland County
Maurice River Township
Heislerville Wildlife Management Area

From Route 47 go southwest just south of Rt. 550 on Rt. 740 and then very soon join Rt. 616, Heislerville-Leesburg Road, also going southwest. Then go west on Rt. 736, Matts Landing Road. Parking is available at the end. Along Matts Landing, I have seen mute swans in a brace of ponds; black ducks, green-winged teal, widgeons, gadwalls, mallards, and pintails also turn up; and Florida gallinule are recorded as having nested about. Further down 616 go west on East Point Road. Early during March the voices of spring peepers will be shrill from the surrounding marshes. Wintering snow geese can almost out-shout you with their massive social crowds. At the end you can park near the historic East Point Lighthouse with its well known red cupola for bird and other watching. Pheasants, quail, and woodcocks are here. According to William J. Boyle, Jr., in his fine book *A Guide to Bird Finding,* you might also on a lucky occasion find in this overall area brown pelicans, white ibis, greater white-fronted geese, black-necked stilts, curlew sandpipers, ruffs, and northern wheatears. He notes least bitterns, yellow-throated, prothonotary, and Kentucky warblers, blue grosbeaks, and orchard orioles as significant nesters.

You could go back to Rt. 616 and go east on it, as Glade Road, for a bit then south on Thompsons Beach Road. Skip this last. The road is incredibly rough and the beach, which seems very inviting on the map, is actually a mess of construction debris as a bulwark levee.

Essex County

Essex County
Essex Fells

The Trotter Tract is located out Oak Lane in the northwestern corner of the borough, just behind and adjoining Northeastern Bible College. This oak woods of many slopes is soft and yellow during autumn and can easily be traversed during an hour or so via dirt roads and leafy trails.

Essex County
West Caldwell Township

In the western corner of town, trails off Passaic Avenue and Parkview Avenue bring you into a more or less open and dry part of the 400-plus acre conservation area known as Hatfield Swamp. The far western border of this flood plain is delimited by the Passaic River, on the other side of which is Morris County. Travelling this stream by canoe is a scenic adventure, entry to be had in Morris County. As you arrive at the swamp from the streets, walk carefully, for your presence will be suddenly revealed as you leave the slender treeline. Sometimes you think you might be able to see a lot here before it slips away, but remember that most of the best will have escape mechanisms built in, such as the extreme slenderness of rails.

Hudson County

Hudson County
Jersey City
Liberty State Park

This 736-acre park along New York Bay stands out for resisting the urban spread that has so come to dominate the banks of the Hudson River. Opening on the Statue of Liberty (to which there are ferries) and Ellis Island, the park has remarkable moments of drama when you catch it in either sunset or sunrise, with the latter time being worth an early rising to meet. Here you will widen your naturalist finds, with sea anemones, bristle worms, fanned worms, acorn barnacles, top shells, moss animals, and sea grapes washing in the brackish waters, sheltering in the salt marsh. American eels and northern pipefish turn up for the wader who seeks a difference.

Get here by taking Exit 14B off the New Jersey Turnpike and following the signs for the park. This means turning left on Bayview Avenue, bearing right at a circle, and then going down Morris Pesin Drive a short distance to the entrance on the right.

For another tidal marsh try Caven Point, just south of Liberty. It is much larger and includes a sandy beach, upland fields, a rock jetty, and magnificent tidal flats. To get here return to the circle and go right toward Jersey City and then almost immediately left on Caven Road. You will come to a U. S. Army guardhouse. If there is a guard, he will probably send you on in to the end, about three-fourths of a mile away and past an estuary worth stopping by.

Hunterdon County

Hunterdon County
Delaware Township
Bull's Island Flood Plain Natural Area

This long slender flat island between the Delaware River and Route 29, where it is separated from the mainland by the Delaware & Raritan Canal, has its entrance from Route 29 just north of Route 519 above Stockton and south of 519 Spur. Bull's Island and Bull's Creek take their names from Richard Bull, one of the first owners of the territory. This canal was the feeder to the Delaware and Raritan Canal which went from Trenton to New Brunswick.

Here in the Natural Area proper, designated and preserved by the State, you will find two unique forest types, the sycamore river birch and the elm-silver maple. Among vines that string off trees spreads one of the largest ostrich fern stands you may see in New Jersey. Along the pebbled shore fronting the Delaware, you will have a window on birdlife as it were. Edge of river species stand out, such as cerulean, parula, prothonotary, and yellow-throated warblers, Acadian flycatchers, phoebes, and cliff swallows. Hawks and occasionally bald eagles sweep past in the open while migrating.

One time I arrived here just after a rain storm, and, as the trees and vines dripped rapidly, I was forced to think of rain forest country. Then, walking down an incline along a path through jewelweeds, I gradually sank out of view as though walking out into the ocean.

Renting of canoes and rowboats is possible nearby. In the Canal you are likely to find catfish, eels, rock bass, and trout. The river offers catfish, rock and smallmouth bass, pickerel, sunfish, suckers, carp, and shad.

Hunterdon County
Holland Township

As you travel, preferably walking or by bike, from east to west down the wooded part of Miller Park Road, in the southeast quadrant of Holland, you will notice that the eastern part is really a hemlock gorge, while the lower outlet is an oak flat. Thus in a distance of just under one mile you will move in two forest regimes. One is much like the hemlock-hardwoods formation of northern Connecticut into Vermont, New Hampshire, and Maine as well as westward. The other represents the great oak lands that extend from the southern border of that territory down into the American southeast.

In these successive forest zones look for microhabitats to bring you different species of birds, wildflowers, and so on as well as contrasting temperatures. The hemlock territory will be cooler and darker through most of the year, so you may find some of the more spectacular varieties of mushrooms, toadstools.

Hunterdon County
Raritan Township

Over on the northeastern side, where River Road parallels the South Branch Raritan River between Route 31 on the north and Bartles Corner Road (Route 612) on the south, a broad slow marsh expands from the current and brings wetlands birds to home. I have parked along a wide shoulder of the unpaved section and looked out across the acres of quiet water and dotting islands of trees, shrubs, and weeds. Here, I have seen in just a few moments great blue herons and great (formerly American) egrets pausing together. Only moments from busy thoroughfares, cries and calls and songs of the open water during summer win the day and often the night.

Hunterdon County
Voorhees State Park

Located in the V between Routes 31 and 513, just north off Route 78, these 515 acres have entrances from both 31 and 513 with that to the park office being from 513.

From 513 you can drive to their scenic overlook and there take a trail through woods up to the observatory. I have not found the observatory open, and I did find the trail often overcrowded with undergrowth, but the encroaching weeds seemed probably a problem only after a rainstorm. In one opening here I found an earthworm midden, a pile of mud gathered together by an earthworm for storing food and letting bacteria and fungi help break it down, into which this simple animal had hauled a section of a red maple leaf.

Campsites, picnic and play areas, and a paracourse fitness circuit expand the use of this attractive park, as does a trail down along Willoughby Brook where I went for sound one early autumn afternoon.

Mercer County

Mercer County
Ewing Township Park

In the northwest corner of Ewing take Bear Tavern Road to the northwest. Aside from picking up Bear Tavern in town, you can take it northwest from an exit off Route 95 where that highway goes between a golf club on its northwest side and the Mercer Airport on its southeast side. From Bear Tavern, make a left at the crossroad Mountainview Road. After about a half mile, you will come on your left to the entrance to this multiple use (tennis courts, bike trail, pond for skating) park. It also has fields and woods and has been designated as a "Wildlife Safety Zone." Here hiking, photography, and nature study are permitted. In the park is a large parking lot, from which you can walk within a few minutes to the farthest reaches of the potentially useful natural parts.

To walk along the towpath of the wooded Delaware and Raritan Canal State Park, take Wilburtha Road north off Route 29 just east of Route 95. This is part of the 60-mile long romantic state park which you will meet again in Lawrenceville, another well-chosen section of the towpath of the canal which opened in 1834. Overall 66 miles of canal and towpaths have been reserved for us.

Mercer County
Hopewell Township

Probably the easiest way to get to the heart of 807-acre rambling Washington Crossing State Park is to take Route 546 north off Route 29 about 8 miles northwest of Trenton. Along 546 you will find the park entrance and shortly later the park office. Farther along 29, you can go right on Church Road and then right again on Brick Yard Road, the latter like other internal roads which it meets brings you to the Nature Center. General George Washington travelled what is now treelined Continental Lane inside the park on his way to defeating the Hessian soldiers in Trenton after he and his Continental Army crossed the Delaware River here on Christmas night, 1776. The war may have turned here.

Today with an arboretum, forest nursery, open-air theater, bike rental, and nature center with trails departing from it, the park offers enough at once so that you would be wise to drop in at the Visitor's Center as soon as possible. For the naturalist the diversity of water, forest, and field makes repeated visits very promising. A patch of ground cedar marks a sideline of one trail. Another path terminates at the edge of an old field that crowns a hill. Back in the summer of 1972, two adjacent plots here, each 100 feet square, were mowed, and one was plowed. You might try to find them and note the changes since then. Also, a wire was stretched in the air diagonally across the plowed field for birds to rest on, with the hope that a comparative study might be made of the crop arising from seeds they dropped. The wire and its poles were later taken down, and a bluebird house put up, but you might try the same exercise in a place of your own.

Mercer County
Lawrence Township

Winding in a fat S between Brunswick Pike and U.S. Route One in the southwest corner of town, Colonial Lake lies in a pleasant suburbs. It attracts ducks and geese and the like and has easy access via the surrounding streets, Lake Drive and Hopatcong Drive. The former has parking places along it and at a park, which has benches and rocks to sit on and a playground. Hopatcong ends in a cul-de-sac at the dammed end of the lake from which you can take macadam foot-paths and follow some channels. Handy for suburban birding for common thicket types such as robins, sparrows, catbirds, and so on, this Green Acres-supported reserve will serve your hunt for wildlife best during off-hours, such as early in the morning.

Slightly over a mile and a half northward on Route One, turn right on Bakers Basin Road. About a thousand feet in, you will come to the park of the Delaware and Raritan Canal, which reaches clear to New Brunswick. From a pull-off on the southeast side you can walk or bike along the towpath up and down this waterway under overarching tree limbs, the direction south being best. This grassy route is part of the unusually long Delaware and Raritan Canal State Park. The park is approximately 60 miles long and provides about as romantic a walk as any in a movie. It is also graced by the songs of birds, with warbling vireos and orchard orioles being a special feature.

Middlesex County

Middlesex County
Old Bridge Township
Cheesequake State Park

This salt marsh habitat takes its name from the Lenni-Lenape Indians. Its many transition lands give you about 450 acres of variety which include along with the marsh, cedar swamps, a lake, ponds, woods, fields, athletic areas, miles of nature trails, campsites, and a beach grass restoration area where mourning doves often turn up, possibly for pebbles.

Owls like to roost in the cedar swamps during the day because it is dark there. They and hawks also choose giant white pines of the uplands where lumbering once supplied white pine trunks to the British and eventually the American navy as masts.

Once while boating out on the salt marsh to look for snowy egrets, which take especially to the smaller creeks, we were following a channel which gradually closed down and forced us to do some backwatering. Quipped my guide, the Park Superintendent, "Well, once in a while you miss," and I settled for a nice photo from the rear of a fast-departing little green heron.

Then on one autumn morning I encountered scores of bank swallows swirling out there while in the woods swarms of gnats jiggled in sunshafts.

Some of the snails here can breath open air and so escape rising saltiness when the tide comes in by climbing up stems to get out of the water.

On another unforgettable occasion, I stood by the shore of the lake and watched in the cold-morning sunlight mist sliding down the slope out onto the still waters.

To get to this expansive park, take Exit 120 (Lawrence Harbor) off the Garden State Parkway and follow the signs. These will put you on Matawan Road going south from which you will quickly turn right on Cliffwood Road and then again right on Gordon Road, which will put you at the park entrance.

Monmouth County

Monmouth County
Colts Neck

Dorbrook Park on the east side offers 380 acres, sanctioned by Green Acres preservation, of athletic fields, woods, open areas, waterfront and swimming (in the Swimming River Reservoir). It straddles Route 537, so go east from Freehold and you will find it a couple of miles past Route 34.

Monmouth County
Eatontown

Eighty-Acre Park on the west side of town off Wall Street provides dirt trails in an oak woods. With their entry off a baseball field, you should be ready for situations of multiple use of the site.

Monmouth County
Freehold Township

At the northern end of town, Durand Park provides a nice woods, openings, and hedgerows atmosphere with some roadside parking available. Travel north on Rt. 537 about 3 miles past its break with Route 79 and turn left (west) on Randolph Road. You can also get on to Randolph by turning east off Route 46. On the south side of Randolph, you will see the little parking place with access to Durand. Walk in carefully so you do not scare up the bobwhite quail before you are ready to see them scaling away. Such diversity of upland habitat promises an orchestra of song in season.

Just south of the 537/79 split, turn west on Old Englishtown Road and then quickly right on Pond Road. About a mile and a half later, you will come on your right to the entrance to Lake Topanemous Park. Here there is parking, swing sets, benches and picnic tables. You can continue walking past these and take a woody pathed walk along the lake and feeding stream. From the path a good view of dipping swallows and swifts can make your day, with a chance for fine photography if you plan for the position of the sun.

Along Route 9, south of the Route 33 interchange, turn west on Adelphia Road. About a mile and a half later turn south on Georgia Road, and less than a mile later you will find on your left the entrance to Liberty Oak Park. This is a large complex of woods, athletic fields, open space, hedgerows, etc., with many parking lots. The variety means something for almost everyone and as much or as little walking with as little or great difficulty as you might wish. Thus people with canes may get almost as much out of it as more mobile sorts.

At the southern end of town, Turkey Swamp County Park offers 512 acres of more or less natural camping, including hot showers and laundry, with a 17-acre manmade lake for swimming, boating, fishing, and ice skating. Camping equipment must, however, be backpacked into the campsites. Nature trails through Pine Barrens habitats of woods, swamps, and bogs are open for you, though you can reserve guided nature walks led by park naturalists by calling ahead of time. An archery range in the adjacent 2,211-acre New Jersey Turkey Swamp Fish & Wildlife Management Area is available, but check for special rules and regulations. A physical fitness trail has been created for various routines, and a soccer field is also present. You can get there off Route 537 by turning south in Smithburg on Route 527, then left about one and one-half miles later on Ely-Harmony Road, left again about one and one-half mile later on Nomoco Road, and finally left about 2 miles farther at the entrance going north on Georgia Road, which Nomoco has joined. From Route 195 take Exit 23 and go north, on Jackson Mills Road and then left on Georgia Road, which will again bring you to the park entrance.

Monmouth County
Freehold and Manalapan Townships
Monmouth Battlefield State Park

The main entrance to this 1,520-acre expanse is on the north side of State Route 33 just west of the Freehold Circle, where State Route 33 and U.S. Route 9 cross. Be sure to go to the Visitor Center for the self-operated slide presentation of the battle. The British were swinging eastward from Philadelphia during the spring of 1778, having heard that the French were moving in to help General Washington's Continental Army. Washington struck all along the 12-mile long British armaments train. Molly Ludwig Hays became famous as "Molly Pitcher" when she carried water to the American troops and then took over her husband's cannon after he became exhausted, all of which brought her both a commendation from the General and an army pension.

After this, the variety and size of the park will be quite fulfilling, offering not only plenty of parking space but even about 25 miles of trails through forest, marsh, and field habitats. Also become alert to the various programs that are put on there. Some of these include year-round wildlife and plant programs at the Owl Haven Nature Center, which is on Route 522 (the Englishtown-Freehold Road)—reachable by park trail but more conveniently by car.

Monmouth County
Howell Township

In the northeastern part of town, a former cranberry bog can be reached off Cranberry Road. Running in an east-west direction along the foot of this wet woods, the bend of the street has a small off the shoulder rough area on its north side where about two cars can pull in.

Manasquan Reservoir has wooded edges which can be followed completely around this large attractive body of open water, since a trail lines the perimeter. Just one glance at the perimeter will tell you that this is heron country, but being basically in the middle of town it will be best examined using binoculars or, better, a telescope. The township requests that you park on the south side where there is an entrance to the reservoir off Windeler Road. This street can be reached easily from Route 195, for instance, by taking Route 9 north and turning right (east) almost immediately on Georgia Tavern Road, with the second right off that being Windeler. If you continue along Georgia Tavern, you will find a small parking lot on the right side; a short walk eastward along the road from here brings you to an opening where you have the reservoir on both sides of the street.

A part of the eastern perimeter of the reservoir is bounded by Manassa Road. At its northeast end it meets Norse Drive, which angles to the southeast. On the north side of Norse you will find a sand and pine land, which you might investigate after parking along the road shoulder.

To the east Norse meets Preventorium Road. Travel south past its crossing of Old Tavern Road, the first crossroad, and on the right enter the athletic fields of Oak Glen Park. Here you will find a Green Acres funded woodland trail which is not only a jogging course but also a reasonable nature trail.

Monmouth County
Marlboro Township

Walking along wooded sandy Igoe Road can be a pleasant transect of an hour or so through this often surprisingly countryish part of New Jersey. Located in the northeast corner of town, Igoe branches off Pleasant Valley Road, which can be taken from County Route 520 (Newman Springs Road) or from Reids Mill Road off N.J. Route 34. The best parking is a hundred yards or so from the northern end since the rest of Igoe is so banked that no shoulders exist.

Monmouth County
Middletown Township

Deep Cut Park, a 40-acre exhibit of gardens and greenhouses of the Monmouth County Park System, has been created for the home gardener. You can get there by taking Laurel Avenue south off Route 35. Turn left on Holland Road and then right on Red Hill Road. The park entrance will be on your left around a bend. You can also leave the Garden State Parkway going one and one-half miles northeast from Exit 114.

Even if you do not go there, you can still ask questions of trained horticulturalists by calling on the Horticultural Hot Line (201) 671-6906. For activites call (201) 671-6050.

Be sure to visit the Horticultural Center for its initial information, library, and gift shop. Then take advantage of its numerous types of gardens, pond, orchard, greenhouses, walks, and so on. Naturally, you can go birding here as well as seek out other forms of nature.

Monmouth County
Ocean Township

Central in the town and bounded to the south by Deal Road and to the east by Whale Pond Road, the Deal Test Site offers a Green Acres funded 208 acres of field, marsh, and woodland. For birders the nature trails may be marred by the presence of a physical fitness trail and a leaf recycling lot. Ancient towers once used for tracking satellites stand as curiosities. All in all, though, once you park, and there is plenty of space for that, and take to the wilds, all can be serene and worth a morning or so.

Monmouth County
Sandy Hook
Gateway National Recreation Area

At least one route here is spectacularly easy: Leave the Garden State Parkway at Exit 105 onto Route 36 and take this east to the marked entrance of Sandy Hook.

Still guarding, as it were, the seasides of northern New Jersey, Staten Island, and New York Harbor, the sandy backbone and inlet curves of this sweeping five-mile long peninsula collects shorebirds all the time, floods of migrants in spring and fall. Here and there a riblike sand bar indicates below the waves ocean currents that show how this big spit with its fresh, intensely green grass was long ago pulled out from the land and still continues to slide beneath almost unexpectedly blue water.

During autumn the line of tinted poison ivy and woodbine leaves along the bank of Plum Island can remind you of early America as seen by settlers coming here. The boardwalk across the road from the Visitor Center leads you out over a salt marsh...bring your binoculars. A Trail Guide exists for The Old Dune Trail.

Historically part of the defense system protecting New York Harbor, Sandy Hook has the nation's oldest continuously operating lighthouse, which has guided shipping since 1764. The roles of Sandy Hook and its old Fort Hancock are told at the Sandy Hook visitor center and Fort Hancock educational offices here now.

For nature and history programs, running all year long, ask at the Visitor Center.

Monmouth County
Tinton Falls Borough

A large wild field lies on the south side of the end of east-running Riverdale Avenue West. In the north end of town, it is easily reached off Rt. 520 (Newman Springs Road) or Rt. 537 and touches Swimming River, adding more variety of habitat. Here, I was able to close to within 20 feet of a mockingbird for a photo, simply because the bird allowed me to walk up to it out in the open.

Morris County

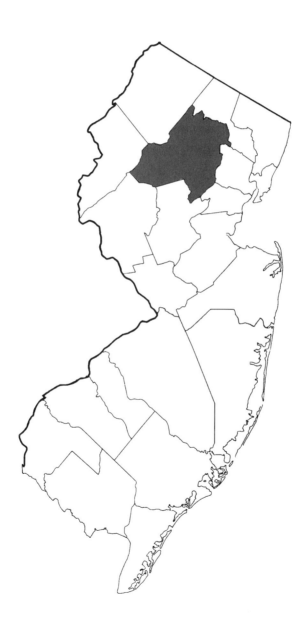

Morris County
Basking Ridge
Great Swamp National Wildlife Refuge

The Refuge Headquarters building is on Pleasant Plains Road. To get here from northbound Route 287, take Exit 30A on to North Maple Avenue. Continue south on this to its union with South Maple and stay south, turning left on Lord Stirling Road. This will become White Bridge Road, from which at the cross-road of Pleasant Plains Road you turn left. The Refuge Headquarters appears shortly on your right.

This sprawling preserve of about 7,000 acres draws more than 200 species of birds into its reasonably pristine nature of swamp, woods, wild fields, and pastures. The most delicate part has been designated the Wilderness Area, roughly the eastern two thirds of the Refuge. Thus there are restrictions here, so please find out what they are.

The remaining third is held for maintaining optimum habitat for wildlife, and so it is identified as the Wildlife Management Area. This you can see from the Wildlife Observation Center and along Pleasant Plains Road.

The eastern side of the Refuge also features an Outdoor Education Center, run by the Morris County Park Commission, with classes and habitat invaluable to the public.

On the western edge of the Refuge is Lord Stirling Park, an Environmental Education Center run by the Somerset County Park Commission, which offers trails, observation blinds, and a number of educational programs.

Morris County
Gladstone

Willowwood Arboretum, in the Hackelbarney Hills of the north-central part of the state, offers 130 rolling acres of wild and cultivated plantings. The variety of specimens (about 3,500 species) and the easy walking adds charm to both individual naturing and attending the classes, workshops, and tours that are conducted here. Notable right away are the many species of oaks, maples, and willows, the elegant Dawn Redwood, and a slope filled with pink ladyslippers. Walking here is so relaxing that you can meander along meditating and suddenly realize hours have passed. Birders will particularly enjoy the openness along the paths, making it easy to follow the travels of a particular bird. Naturally, this also enhances photographing.

This part of the Morris County Park System can be reached by taking Daly Road (just north of Rt. 512) west off Route 206 and then turning right on Longview Road, with the arboretum entrance quickly to your left.

Bamboo Brook Outdoor Education Center, also part of the Morris County Park System and listed in Chester Township, is right next door. A sharp geologic change occurs here. A large part of Bamboo Brook rests on rock of the Highlands Province, while Willowbrook is on rock of the Piedmont Province. You can get to the Bamboo Brook entrance simply by going a bit farther on Longview Road.

Morris County
Jefferson Township

Located along Weldon Road, the 1300-acre Mahlon Dickerson Reservation can be reached from Route 23 by taking Oak Ridge Road south. It becomes Berkshire Valley Road. You turn right on Ridge Road and left on Schoolhouse Road. At its end you turn right on Russia Road and then left on Weldon to the entrance on the left side, where you will find the Education Center. Weldon also leaves Route 15, which itself has gone north for about five miles from Exit 34 of Route I-80.

Ponds, a large swamp, a hemlock grove with solitary vireos, a bog, an overlook from which you can see Lake Hopatcong, numerous hiking trails, and places for trailers and tents make this wooded country reserve attractive to naturalists. Birders will enjoy looking for wild turkeys, broad-winged hawks, and others which breed here.

Morris County
Kinnelon Borough

To reach Silas Condict Park from Route 23, take Route 618 south and then William Lewis Arthur Drive to the right, the entrance to this 265-acre part of the Morris County Park System.

Hiking trails abound and reach several scenic overlooks of the New Jersey Highlands. Coming at the right time, you may also find wildlife in and around the seven-acre lake. There are also other entertainments such as ball playing and horseshoeing, and you may even want to try ice fishing.

Morris County
Morris, Harding, and Chatham Townships

Taking Route 24 east from Morristown Town, turn south on Loantaka Way. This road goes through the lower third of the Morris County park known as the Loantaka Brook Reservation. Here on your right you will find an entrance and parking lot for this part of the Morris County Park System.

In these 574 acres, you will find stables, softball fields, a picnic area, and a trail used by hikers, bikers, and cross-country skiers. In fact the park is so devoted to trailing that about five miles of paved trails exist here. The "Helen Hartley Jenkins" Woods are reserved for bicycling, hiking, horseback riding, and even deer watching. They have a special attraction in Loantaka Brook that courses through the park, giving it its linear form and ultimately helping feed Great Swamp National Wildlife Refuge just to the south.

The name "Loantaka" comes from two Lenni-Lenape Indian words which mean "the place of the cold winter." Appropriately, one of my most pleasurable experiences here was one autumn day after most tree leaves had fallen. I discovered on a number of beech trees, normally evidences of cold territories, a coating of sooty smut. Branches and remnant leaves were cloaked with this black fungus as with a kind of coalminer's snow.

Morris County
Morris, Harding, and Mendham Townships

The several miles of hiking trails in Lewis Morris Park, an 1,154-acre part of the Morris County Park System, can be reached via two entrances that cut directly off the south side of Route 24 in Morris Township about 3 miles west of Morristown. Just west of those openings you can take Corey Lane south to Tempe Wick Road and turn left. Almost a mile down Tempe Wick on the left is a road to a parking place with restrooms, parking, and overnight camping facilities, all in Mendham Township. You can also go as far again and then left again on Jockey Hollow Road, which puts you into Jockey Hollow National Park, from which you can again enter the main body of Lewis Morris.

Strong on multiple use, the park facilities of deciduous woods and open areas include a Cultural Center, camping sites, swimming, softball fields, sledding and ski touring, and hiking trails, all combining to give you large variety in naturing.

Morris County
Morristown

The 127-acre George Griswold Frelinghuysen Arboretum, part of the Morris County Park System, is fortunately for you very close to Interstate 287. If you are travelling north on 287, leave at Exit 32A. You will be on Morris Avenue. Stay in the middle lane for about half a mile, then bear left, on Whippany Road. At the second traffic light make a backwards left turn, on East Hanover Avenue. About one quarter of a mile up this, on your left and across from the Morris County Free Library, is the entrance to the Arboretum.

Coming south on 287, leave at Exit 32, following the signs for Ridgedale Avenue. Go right on the exit ramp and drive to the first traffic light, then go right onto Ridgedale Avenue. At the second traffic light on Ridgedale turn right, onto East Hanover Avenue. About a quarter of a mile farther, you will find the entrance to the Arboretum on your right, across from the Morris County Free Library.

Now the headquarters of the Morris County Park Commission, the property has numerous nature trails, including a Braille one, that wind among cultivated collections of trees and shrubs which are arranged elegantly for both educational and scientific uses. A number of exotic species also grow here, such as the Blue Atlas Cedar with its seemingly sculptured cones, more familiar to people in its native North African Atlas Mountains. With a large Education Center, the Arboretum offers lectures and workshops for all ages throughout the year. Of course you yourself can treat the grounds simply as a large natural area. The huge variety of plants promises a world of insect species which have their own specific requirements.

Morris County
Mountain Lakes Borough
Boonton and Denville Townships

The 495 acres of forested Tourne Park, part of the Morris County Park System, can be reached from Route 287 by going north and taking exit 34. At the end of the ramp make a left, and then at the first stop light go right on Fanny Road. Go to the second stop sign and turn right on The Boulevard. One quarter of a mile later make a left on Powerville Road. Continue here to your first left, McCaffery Lane, which is the access road to Tourne Park.

Here are picnic and recreation areas but also excellent hiking. There are wildflower and hemlock trails, the wildflower one being on the right 0.4 miles in from the main entrance and the hemlock trail taking you through a notable grove of hemlocks. Also in the park are some very good trails for sledding and crosscountry skiing. One especially rugged trail will twist through forested rock outcroppings to a summit from which you can see the skyline of New York City. Thus the name "Tourne" comes from Dutch and appropriately means "lookout" or "mountain."

Morris County
Parsippany-Troy Hills

Old Troy Park, of the Morris County Park System, can be reached off Reynolds Avenue in the Township of Parsippany-Troy Hills. Reynolds goes north from Route 10, just east of the crossing of Route 511.

The 96 acres include a number of recreation points, but for naturing the paths and trails will offer the best attraction. Here more than 30 species of warblers have been counted late in summer. The Acadian and yellow-bellied flycatchers and summer tanager also bring out the more dedicated birders.

Morris County
Rockaway Township

Up in the highlands in the northeastern part of town, Mt. Hope Pond offers parking along Mt. Hope Road on its northern side and also at the sandy beach to the south. From its wooded shores you peer out as upon a sudden jewel discovered by chance. It has been stocked with trout and small-mouthed bass, but because of insurance rates no boating is allowed.

More centrally, along Shake Hill Road, Lake Ames invites from two fair-sized parking lots off the paved road. Deep in the woods, Ames has Green Acres input. A tot lot near the upper parking lot and a swing set near the lower invite the youngest children. Swans out on the lake suggest suburbia, but its marshy and craggy outlines, darkened by tall trees bring in the naturalist. Siltiness of the water has diminished its quality for drinking and other use, and so the visitors center up the road is closed. That probably enhances the natural aspects of the overall lakeside experience.

Toward the northeastern end of town, Timberbrook Road east and north of Jacobs Road takes you for a rocky but hospitable walk through an elegant old oak forest. One can use a 4-wheel to drive its more tumultuous aspects, notably to the north of Winnebago Scout Reservation, but otherwise walking is the best way to travel here where the tumult and the shouting are soon left far behind.

Down in the southeast an area of about 600 acres, put aside by the State to demonstrate herbaceous plant life which grows along small streams in contrast to the overlording hardwood forest, can be found adjoining the northern border of the Splitrock Reservoir. Get here by walking eastward from Splitrock Road near its meeting with Upper Hibernia Road. You can reach Upper Hibernia at its northern end by taking it east from Route 513 (which itself has come north at Exit 37 of Route 80) and then turning south, with Splitrock Road eventually splitting off to the left.

Morris County
Washington Township

Located right in the center of town, the 530-acre Schooley's Mountain Park of the Morris County Park System has a number of visiting facilities based on open, wooded, and lakeside use for the public. Ball fields, swimming, and boating make for a wider family interest, but there is plenty of territory and trails for hiking and thus some wilderness experience. To get there take Springtown Road north from Route 24, and you will find the entrance on your right.

In the extreme southeastern corner of town, paved Black River Road parallels the forested rocky Black River for enough of a mile and with enough pulloffs for a group to get a good look at wildlands stream living. This part of Black River also gains from Hacklebarney State Park which adjoins on the north. The stream bed is flat enough so that you can walk it comfortably with everyday boots. Enough of the stones are small so that you can also lift and look under them; doing so with a seine downstream, you can get a good estimate of the kinds and numbers of riffle-dwelling aquatic animals here, such as crayfish and johnny darters. Similarly easily accessible ponded places lend themselves to a look at that sort of quieter living quarters.

Morris County
Washington and Chester Townships
Hacklebarney State Park

These scenic 569 acres, built around the gorge of the Black River (more on this under Washington Twp. itself), can be easily reached by turning south on Hacklebarney State Park Road from Route 24 just west of the 24 intersection with Route 206. The park entrance will be just over a mile down the road on your right.

Here you will find the State-designated Natural Area of about 275 acres, characterized by the boulder-strewn gorge of first Trout Creek and then the tumbling Black River. Hemlocks and mixed hardwoods such as oaks and maples darken Hacklebarney during summer, brighten it with green and yellow during autumn. Here is a place to come and listen to Louisiana waterthrushes down near the running waters, low flying hooded warblers up among their nests in a line of mountain laurels. Under broken and stream-worn rocks crayfish and darters stay back during flood times so as not to be hurled downstream. Trout and other fish are stocked every year.

Morris County
Wharton Borough

A gentle walk in an oak woods makes for a pleasurable hike westward out Stirling Street down in the southwest corner of town. This and the adjoining multiple use park, which means you want to be aware of the date and time during which you go birding here, are supported by Green Acres funding.

Morris County
other places in Essex and Hunterdon Counties
East Hanover—Washington Townships

Patriots' Path is a network of hiking trails, bikeways, and open spaces that links a number of municipal, county, and Federal parks as well as other places in Morris, Essex, and Hunterdon Counties. For a map of the Morris County section contact the Morris County Park Commission, P.O. Box 1295, 53 East Hanover Avenue, Morristown, NJ 97962-1295.

Ocean County

Ocean County
Bass River
Great Bay Boulevard Wildlife Management Area

About 4,670 acres of salt marsh country awaits the visitor here, with even an occasional bald eagle migrating through. The overall area is known to many people as the Tuckerton Marshes or just Tuckerton. The township of Tuckerton lies along Route 9, and from town you take Great Bay Boulevard, or Seven Bridges Road, south. Driving down this road, you will cross five bridges, some agonizingly narrow and planked, with potholes in between as you aim for the termination five miles away at Little Egg Inlet.

Once in a while you will find the edges good places to hunt for conch shells. When the tide is out, numerous shorebirds hunt through the mudflats. Fishermen find striped bass, weakfish, fluke, flounder, white perch, sea bass, sharks, and bluefish in the bays and estuaries.

Ocean County
Bass River State Forest
Absegami Trail Natural Area

This land of pine barrens and white-cedar bog consists of about 17,645 acres of state park with recreational facilities, attractive Lake Absegami, and about 100 acres of Natural Area reserved by New Jersey to demonstrate southern bog habitats. Bounded on the south by Stage Road and on the east by Millie Road and the Garden State Parkway, Absegami with its park office and campgrounds is easily reached off Stage Road, which meets U.S. Highway 9 on its north side about seven miles east of New Gretna. The park proper can be reached going south on the GSP by leaving at Exit 52 and going north on Route 654 to its meeting with Stage Road, from which signs will guide you. Heading north on GSP leave at Exit 50 and take Route 9 into New Gretna, where you make a left on Route 679, going toward Chatsworth. In about a mile and a half go right, as 679 goes left, then turn right on Stage Road and use the signs.

The self-guided nature walk is about a half-mile long. The word "Absegami" comes from the same Algonquin Indian word as "Absecon," apparently meaning "The Place of the Swans." Such a designation fits the overall greater area only, although along the trail you will probably see and hear many kinds of birds typical of the Pine Barrens and of east coast migration patterns. Here and there the nature trail is crossed by game trails, which you will notice as slender defiles in the grass and weeds.

Ocean County, Berkeley/Lacey Townships
Double Trouble State Park

This entry to the Pinelands has so much variety that you may want to schedule a whole day for walking here.

The quickest way to pinpoint the entrance is to take Exit 80 off the southbound lane of the Garden State Parkway (note: there is no Exit 80 off the northbound lane), turn left (south) on Double Trouble Road, which parallels the GSP, and continue to its end, about 3 miles down a mostly pleasantly wooded drive. You meet Pinewald/Keswick Road, and right across it is the park entrance to 5,143 acres of oak-pine forest, Atlantic white cedar swamps, cranberry bogs, the Platt Reservoir, and more. Buildings of the former sawmill operation remain, and from people there came the original answer to muskrats chewing holes in the dams, namely "Trouble!" When two such holes appeared in one week, the natural epithet was, "Double trouble!"

You can follow your own way or perhaps take a self-guided nature trail where benches are conveniently available. Nature-seeking during October, you may even run into farmers harvesting cranberries on leased land. Open water at any time can be fished, often profitably for sunfish and eastern chain pickerel. The middle of May is particularly choice under the sweetbay magnolias of Magnolia Lane. Old fashioned wild rice is easily seen upstream from the bridge over Cedar Creek. Just to your right you can see also the 56-acre Mill Pond Bog, now elegantly sinking under nature's return to this once developed land.

On one misty day late in December, I felt particularly attuned to dark scabs of black knot on wild cherry branches, a fungal infection, dangerous to the plant, that can be gummy but which that day was crusted. Along the same path dead gray birches spewed out birch polypore fungi, fleshy platters that stuck out like smoky tan wads of bubble gum which had frozen as if horizontal tongues. That they are used to keep a campfire going and act in anesthesia adds a brightening woodland flavor to something which is mostly noticed for potentially identifying birch, living or dead, from a distance.

The scene seemed even more gothic when a number of the scrub oaks identified themselves as oaks by the woody lumps that were weighing down branches. Gouty oak galls, they were an inch or so in diameter and suggested small but hefty clubs. They are made by the larvae of minute wasps, the holes in them indicating where the adults have exited, and have another part of their life cycle in blister galls on oak leaves.

A more thorough write-up on this park can be found in the piece "Want to Get Into Trouble? Double Trouble?" by naturalist Brian Vernachio in *New Jersey Audubon* magazine for Winter 1996-97 (Vol. 22, No. 4, pp. 20-22).

Ocean County
Brick Township
Swan Point Natural Area

A salt marsh habitat of about 147 acres located at the northern limit of the Barnegat Bay ecosystem, this is another good example of the value of Green Acres funding. Such preserves are a necessary part of the ever-diminishing territory left for migrant birds of the Atlantic Flyway.

Ocean County
Island Beach State Park
Island Beach Research Area and Wildlife Sanctuary

Along the east coast of New Jersey and about 50 miles north of Atlantic City, Island Beach State Park is a ten mile long barrier beach, or offshore bar, that averages just under half a mile in width, and occupies a territory of about 2,694 acres. That the whole belonged to Lord Stirling back in the seventeenth century, when it was known as Lord Stirling's Isle, informs you of the size of some early English estates north of the southern plantations. On the west you meet Barnegat Bay, fed by Toms River and others, and on the east is the Atlantic Ocean, which washes the public beach area as well as that of the sanctuary. Basically the land vegetation is undisturbed, with that of the sanctuary most untouched. You can get there by taking Route 37 east and then Route 35 south to the park entrance, where you pay a small fee.

About 1,200 acres of the southern end of the park, 3.3 miles long and the whole width of the park, the preserve proper brings you a long view of sand dune ecology.

Shortly after entering the park, you will come to a set of small buildings, the one on the left being the Aeolium Nature Center. Here are exhibits and a staff which offers free guided tours. Also, you can walk through a brief self-guided nature trail into dune country. Here as elsewhere you will be asked to take particular care of the beach heather, Hudsonia, and beach grass; they tie down the sand of the dunes.

Autumn can be a particularly nice time to walk here, for then the beach plums are ripe and the trees, shrubs, and vines are going colorful. Seaside goldenrod brings the yellows of summer going into autumn; feel how rubbery its leaves are, thicker as a protection against the constant salt spray. Birds plod and skitter along the beach more often now that people are few. Not only are the plums delicious, especially after a few hours of roaming the sea front, but they make an excellent jelly. The mists and fine salt spray of some mornings might make you think of the first people to land here, unaware of the gigantic continent ahead.

Ocean County
Lakewood Township

Lying just north of Route 70 along Route 9, Lakewood is helped with its name by having two county parks and one township park, all containing lakes. As you go up Route 9, turn right on Route 88, and you will quickly pass between the two county properties.

On the north side of 88 is one called simply Ocean County Park or Ocean County Park No. 1. Having about 323 acres of almost every sort of recreational area imaginable, except perhaps one for boating, this highly developed park lies mostly under tall deciduous trees, giving it a very forested atmosphere made unusual for the number of tree and shrub species, over 150, here. The deer brought in also help. In a sense, then, it provides the best in suburbanized nature. And no wonder, for John D. Rockefeller once lived here.

Just across the highway south is Lake Shenandoah Park, about 143 acres of open land, dominated by its center piece, 50-acre Lake Shenandoah. Stocked and naturally inhabited with about 26 species of fish, it of course offers fishing to the public. At the same time this introduced body of water has become valuable to original nature. Species of herring have long spawned in the south branch of the Metedeconk River. Now many also climb a fish ladder to Shenandoah and use it as a nursery for their young.

Following Route 9 north, turn right on Route 526, East County Line Road. Just over a mile down and on your left is the entrance to Lakewood Pine Park. This small woodsy tract does have nature trails to go with its athletic bent. Just east of this entrance, take Hope Chapel Road south and then go left on North Lake Drive, then right on Case Road and quickly left on Lake Park. These roughly parallel wooded Lake Carasaljo and its western feeder. Here and there are places you can pull off and walk along a trail near the water. Similarly on the south side is South Lake Drive, along which are number of pull-offs.

Ocean County
Manahawkin Wildlife Management Area
Manahawkin Natural Area

This is about 64 acres of mature bottomland hardwood forest in the 965 acres of the Management Area, a National Natural Landmark. The preserve lies along a spur north of and parallel to Route 72 just southeast of Route 9, with Stafford Avenue piercing in off the spur, and is bounded on the east by Cedar Creek. Just remember that this is a Wildlife Management Area, so be careful during hunting seasons.

Here you will find deer, quail, grouse, woodcocks, among others. The ponds attract black ducks, mallards, widgeon, teal, and others and contain largemouth bass. If black rails have returned, search for them late in May or early in June, walking carefully by night in the salt marsh. Listen for the high-pitched "Kee-kee-kerr" call which might be heard from as far as a mile away. Cedar Creek, which you can get to from Stafford Avenue, gives you crabs, white perch, snapper blues, and eels.

Ocean County
Manchester Wildlife Management Area

Two miles north of Route 70 on Route 539 turn right on Horicon Road. About 1.4 miles down on your left you will find a pull-off for parking. From here as elsewhere along the road you can investigate this 2,376-acre forest of pitch pines and scrub oaks with cedar swamp lowland and a managed five-acre field.

As usual with wildlife management areas, be careful during hunting seasons. You will find that hedgerows for food and cover are maintained for deer, rabbits, grouse, quail, and released wild turkeys—which naturally makes these acres prime property for you to observe these species!

Ocean County
Plumsted and Jackson Townships
Colliers Mills Wildlife Management Area

Open from 5 a.m. to 9 p.m., this 12,250 acre tract of fields, woods, and white cedar swamp has six ponds and a wide variety of wildlife, which includes the Pine Barrens Treefrog and, right at the entrance, orchard orioles nesting near the bridge. You can get there by taking Route 528 eastward from Route 537, crossing over Route 539 in Plumsted Township, Ocean County and meeting the area at the next crossroads, Prospertown-Colliers Mills Road (Hawkin Road). There is plenty of parking here.

Out in the fields you will find bluebird houses and, in season, sign of the occupants. In a red maple swamp look for northern waterthrushes, about as far south in New Jersey as you will find them nesting. A rare find, so far not since the 1930s, would be red and white-winged crossbills nesting in the Area.

Be alert that this is a Wildlife Management Area and is available to hunters in season.

Salem County

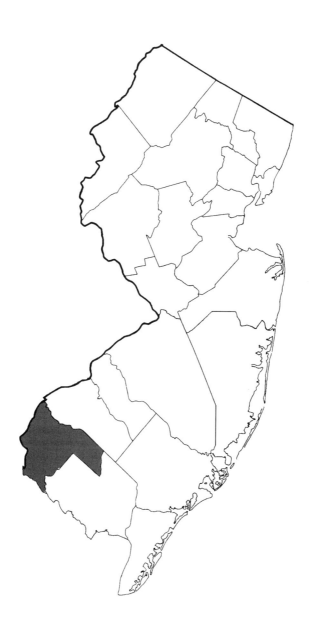

Salem County
Alloway Township

On Mowers Station Road, a fairly wide dirt lane of about 1.2 miles in length, you will pass a landfill and some open fields to your right as you travel through oak woods. These are property of the Salem County Utilities Authority, while the woods to your right are privately owned—and occupied during hunting season by numbers of hunters. Park on the Utilities side shoulder and enjoy a country walk.

You can reach this area by going south on East Lake Road off Route 40 just east of Woodstown Borough. Turn left where East Lake ends at Alloway Road and then soon right on Fenwick Road. Take Fenwick south to Swedes Bridge Road, where Fenwick ends as Oechsle Road. Now turn left on Swedes Bridge toward McKillip which Swedes Bridge crosses and becomes Mowers Station Road.

Swedes Bridge Road can also be taken east from the Mannington Township border.

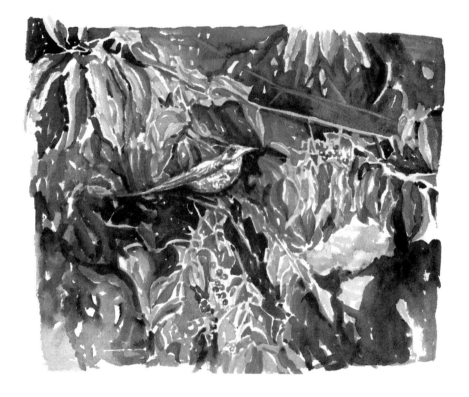

Salem County
Downe Township
Fortesque Wildlife Management Area

In the southwest corner of the state off Route 553, take Rt. 732 west and then Rt. 637 south through salt marshes to its end on New Jersey Avenue. Here, you will find a narrow sandy beach along Delaware Bay. Snow geese collect down here, a place where I saw my first marsh hawk as it tilted low over weeds in a misty rain. Banks of hollies down Route 637, Fortesque Road, promise birds from the fruiting season on, and mourning cloak butterflies emerge from hibernating even by the first of March. Also on these 900 acres you will find quail, black ducks, widgeon, teal, gadwall, and others. In the tidal creeks crabs crawl, while out in Delaware Bay it is worth looking for weakfish, fluke, sea bass, and black drum.

Salem County
Downe Township
Gandy's Beach

In the southwestern corner of the state off Route 553, take Rt. 732 west to Rt. 637 south, then right at the fork on Rt. 643, continuing to its end at the beach. After crossing through a large salt marsh area, bear left on Gandy Avenue and then left along the beach. At an opening in the snow fence near summer homes you will be able to walk on the sand of a wide attractive beach.

Salem County
Elmer

On the east side of Elmer and on the north border of Route 40, Elmer Lake offers a small park with fireplaces, athletic fields, and a view through wetland trees and cattails of enough open water that a brief birding trip is possible. It is best if you get here before the crowd.

Salem County
Fairfield
Dix Wildlife Management Area

In the southwestern corner of the state take Route 601, Back Neck Road, to its end southwest off Route 553. Here are 2,494 acres of marshland, field, and forest where you will find black ducks, mallards, pintails, geese, grouse, quail, pheasants, woodcocks, deer, and so on. In the waters, striped bass and white perch are common.

Salem County
Lower Alloways Creek Township

In the City of Salem, drop south off Route 49 on Salem-Hancocks Bridge Road. After about two miles turn left on Hancocks Bridge-Quinton Road. Right after you cross New Bridge Road, you will enter a small marsh-swamp that is part of Alloways Creek immediately to the south. On the north side of the road the wetland is swamp thicket, on the south side marsh phragmites. You can park a few cars along the road shoulder.

Continue for about two and one-half miles down New Bridge Road, which becomes Harmersville-Canton Road, and turn left on Friendship Road, then very soon right on Buckhorn Road. About a half mile along, Buckhorn crosses a tributary to Stow Creek. Here you can park for waterfowl watching from the road. Continue on a bit and near the end of a farmfield on the right the road becomes dirt, and you enter a woods. Here begins over a half mile of woodland walking among lovely oaks after you park on the shoulder.

Farther on up Friendship Road turn right on Hell Neck Road. Just over a mile out on the right is a gravel pit that is largely rimmed by woods, good birding habitat and nesting for killdeer.

Farther up Friendship after Hell Neck Road is the Maskells Mill Pond Wildlife Management Area, which can be seen under that title in the following pages.

Also nearby are roads and trails into the Mad Horse Creek Fish and Wildlife Management Area. Two places stand out in this 5,826-acre wilds, both of them basically tidal marshlands. To get to the first, which ends up a drive on a dirt road through scrub woods and tall phragmites with a number of parking places, take Salem-Hancocks Bridge Road south off Route 49 in the City of Salem into the Village of Hancocks Bridge. Here take any side street after Front Street to the right and keep bearing right until you link up with Alloway Creek Neck Road. Follow this highway south—through fields which may flood over in spring and draw migrating ducks and shorebirds—for about two and a half miles. Once in this scrub country, you will take a dirt road to the left. This forms a loop through mostly upland territory. During hunting season this wild property attracts a number of hunters for quail, pheasant, and rabbits, as well as waterfowl, so beware.

The second spot has trickier directions but is worth it for the view out onto the Delaware Bay and its waterfowl. Take Salem-Hancocks Bridge Road past Hancocks Bridge village, bearing left and then right where Cuff Road splits off to the left. Keep swinging right and your route becomes Harmersville-Canton Road. This you take south, turning right on Long Bridge Road. It in turn ends at Stow Neck Road, and you turn left. Stow Neck is a long wavering highway which is a good place to go in winter when looking for rough-legged hawks and marsh hawks.

The road terminates in a parking lot on Pine Island of pitch and loblolly pine, various oaks, and evergreen American holly. This is a place where you might find boat-tailed grackles, which have finally arrived this far north. Here there are boat ramps for public use and a fine view out over the water. Striped bass and white perch are common in the saltwaters of both the Bay and streams here.

Salem County
Lower Alloways Creek Township
Maskells Mill Pond Wildlife Management Area

Travelling south on Salem-Hancocks Bridge Road from Route 49 in the City of Salem, bear left as the road becomes Hancocks Bridge-Harmersville Road and proceed straight through the intersection of this with New Bridge Road. Your route is now Maskells Mill Road, which you follow for about a mile, with the entry to and parking for Maskells Mill Pond turning up on your left soon after you pass Cross Road also on your left. The 47 acres are dominated by a 33-acre pond, which drains over a dam near your parking place. Here you will find good fishing of chain pickerel, yellow bullheads, pumpkinseed, bluegills, and American eels; with luck you might also catch some largemouth bass, black crappies, and carp. Just remember that only cartop boats and electric motors are permitted and that only about ten percent of the shoreline is available for fishing from the bank.

Salem County
Mannington Township
Mannington Marsh and environs

This large tidal marsh sprawls conveniently across a number of highways, making it very accessible. I usually get there from farther north by taking Exit 2B off the south-going lanes of State Route 295 down near the Delaware Memorial Bridge and proceeding eastward on Route 40 and then going basically southeastward on Route 540. Within a couple of miles, it crosses Mannington's Griscom Road, which to both right and left touches good birding spots of the marsh, as does 540 here also.

You can also take Route 45 southwest from Route 40. You will cross the marsh just after the second juncture with Compromise Road. Then, too, Route 49 northwestward out of Salem meets Route 45, and here you turn right, now to touch the marsh just after the right juncture of the Quinton-Mannington Hill Road.

Just south of the marsh, Route 45 joins both northgoing routes 540 and 620, Griscom Road ending here at Route 620.

Both 540, or Pointers Auburn Road, and 620, or Pointers Swedesboro Road, cross the marsh, and they, along with Route 45, give you fine birding spots.

As autumn deepens, you will find the low rolling farmlands with their wide vales being swept by flocks of migrating red-winged blackbirds and grackles. During spring notice how male grackles tilt their tails up into a lumplike V, a sexual display. Cattle egrets are buffy of back; in Africa they are called the "buff-backed heron." Look closely, and you may find the beaks bloodred as they are during their mating season.

Out on the marsh I have seen mute swans nesting on the tops of muskrat houses. As they wing overhead, listen for the creaking sort of singing coming from their wings, remindful of the music from hurtling mourning doves.

Huge American Lotuses (*Nelumbo*), water-lilies, blossom massively along the edge of the marsh. During autumn and spring you may find these colonies equally unusual for their giant pyramidal seedpods.

Just northeast of the juncture of 620 (Pointers Swedesboro Road) and Griscom stands a house on the east side of 620. Hugh Middleton, a member of the provincial legislature and a judge of the court, built this place in 1735. Evidently power-seeking, he was regarded by the opposition as trying "to run all of New Jersey."

Taking Route 45 northeast, you will find Cheney Road on your right just before the Pilesgrove Township border. Also on the right at this juncture is the Vo-Tech Career Center. Down Cheney Road a few hundred yards is the New Jersey Regional School of Mannington to your left, and just beyond that, bordering it, is a small woods. A short grassy driveway leads off Cheney, and you can park there. An entry has been cut into this oak island and developed as a picnic cul-de-sac.

195

Salem County
Oldmans Township

Taking Exit 7 east off Route 295, you will enter the flat farm country of Oldmans. Make your first left, from Straughns Mill Road (Rt. 643) onto Perkintown Road (Rt. 644), and very quickly on your left you will pass the fencing that bounds a property which holds a large farm pond. During migration seasons especially, park along the roadside and with binoculars watch the waterfowl there. During one autumn I noticed over 100 at once floating on the surface like ships at rest.

You will find a similar sort of population of birds on a broad marsh to the west. Take Straughns Mill west from Rt. 295, then your first right (Freed Road), then right again as Freed ends on Pedricktown-Woodstown Road (Rt. 602). Almost immediately you will cross the marsh, and you can park either along the shoulder or take your next right (Seminole Road) and park near the public swim club at the end.

Salem County
Parvin State Park
Parvin Natural Area

Off Route 540 near its juncture with Route 553, this lake, stream, and forested reserve of about 500 acres has camping facilities that make it accessible for enjoying night in an oak-pine woods. A footpath along its Muddy Run creek takes you through a winding shallow gorge that is a pleasure at any season. During winter it can be of exceptional interest to the photographer for the perched ice which is left behind as the stream changes its depth. On an autumn afternoon I watched a long snake weaving almsot languidly upstream, but it nosed ashore before I could identify it. Still I was "lucky" enough to be on the uplands one summer night when a small fire got out of control briefly and was only several hours later quelled by fire engines which reeled about agilely in the woods.

Once small ponds were created in the area by dams to create power for sawmills and gristmills. It will not surprise you that a family named Parvin owned one such operation.

With care you may encounter such mammals as raccoons, opossums, skunks, weasels, muskrats, foxes, wood mice, and deer. Occasionally a snake will wander up the creek, its weaving wake making it easy to detect from a distance. Birders will enjoy the prospect of seeing prothonotary warblers and summer tanagers, usually more familiar in areas further south. Swallows close the evening over the two lakes, Parvin and Thundergust, while whippoorwills bring on the night with their throaty music. One whippoorwill rolled out its calls 1088 times with barely a pause, wrote naturalist John Burroughs. If you catch one in the beam of your flashlight, you may find its eyes glowing a bright orange.

Salem County
Pennsville
Fort Mott State Park

Near the northern terminus of Route 49 in the southwestern part of New Jersey, take Fort Mott Road, Rt. 630, southwest (or Lighthouse Road northwest to Fort Mott road and turn left at the juncture) to the park. Here on 104 acres, you will find a broad lawn with picnic tables and benches as well as a bunker as a further lookout. State boundaries are such that if you walk out past the low tide line you will be in Delaware, a fact that may help you set up and win some bets about being in that state from New Jersey without using boat, plane, bridge, or whatever. Aside from watching shore birds and seeing Pea Patch Island, you can also get a long slow view of ships travelling the Delaware River.

Salem County
Pennsville Township

On the west side of Route 49, Cedar Point Park offers a view out on the Delaware River. People come here simply to watch the ships ease by. I tend to lean against a rail, binoculars in hand, and watch some of the shorebirds from above. Early in the morning is best for simple viewing; late afternoon means you will have a backlit subject as the sun gives you one last strong, but not unfriendly, stare.

Salem County
Pilesgrove Township

Travelling eastward along Route 40, turn north on the Pointers-Auburn Road, the western border of Pilesgrove and the eastern border of Oldmans Township. Your first right will be Featherbed Lane, which terminates at Kings Highway. Just before this ending, look to the right at the farm pond a few hundred yards away. Migrating waterfowl pause here. Swallows dip to catch insects and to drink on the wing. Migrating grackles, blackbirds, cowbirds, and starlings wing among the cows along the fencing on the other side of the road. In his fine book *A Guide to Bird Finding in New Jersey* William J. Boyle, Jr., notes that on June 2, 1982, that someone saw a scissor-tailed flycatcher here. Hopefully, the bird was a male, and the observer got to see its aerial gymnastics during a courtship display.

Farther east along Route 40, turn left on Harrisonville Lake Road. About two and one-half miles up it, you will cross a ponded area which is the border with Harrisonville. You can park here for birdwatching.

Back on Route 40 going east, turn right (south) at the immediate crossroad, Avis Mill Road, and park about a half mile down it for more birds down in the draw at Avis Mill Pond.

Somerset County

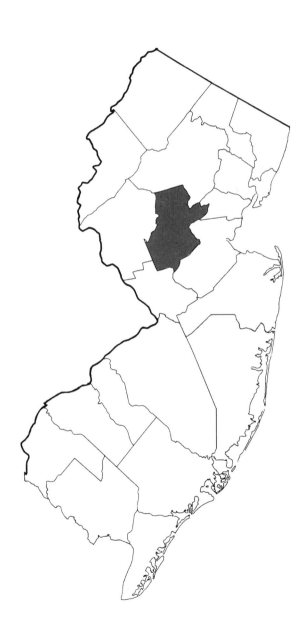

Somerset County
Bernardsville, Basking Ridge,
and Harding Township
Scherman-Hoffman Sanctuaries

To reach the Hoffman building, which houses the Sanctuary offices, directors, and various other services from Route 287, take Exit 30B and go northwest on North Maple Avenue. Continue through the traffic light onto Childs Road from which you soon bear right at a fork onto Hardscrabble Road. In about one mile you will find the Sanctuary driveway; the parking lot is about 1/4 of a mile up that. The whole route is made much easier by the signs that say NJ Audubon Center.

About 260 acres of woods, grassy openings, and flowing waters give this combined project ecological and topographical variety. Walks along the 3.2 miles of trails have a tone of intimacy and warmth. Thus you will find here a strong array of educational programs.

From the Scherman parking lot you can reach Patriot's Path, worth travelling since its expanse links various aspects of natural interest to the north in Morris County.

Sussex County

Sussex County
Flatbrook-Roy Wildlife Management Area

From Route 206 about 6 miles north of Branchville, take Rt. 560 west and then about a mile and a half later Rt. 615 to your left. You will have only about a mile of wildlife habitat available along the road, for it ends with an out bridge. Still, several grassy roads, such as one into a grove of white pines, and a parking lot give you access to the 2,334 acres of fields and wooded uplands. Trout are stocked in both Big and Little Flat Brooks.

Sussex County
Fredon and Green Townships
Whittingham Natural Area

This 400 acres of northern swamp and floodplain, surrounded by a 1,114-acre wildlife management area for upland game and deer, is dedicated to being a refuge for wildlife, especially beavers and otters. Just south of Newton and west of Route 206, the overall site is bounded to the west by Route 319, which comes off northern east-west Route 519 and becomes Route 608 to the south, and then joins east-west Route 611, Springdale & Tranquillity Road. On the northeastern corner it is traversed for over two miles by Springdale Road, which crosses Route 519 and meets Route 618, Springdale and Fredon Road, which bounds this corner for about two miles. One way of reaching it is from the 206 exit (No. 25) off Route 80. Take 206 about nine miles south to Route 618, Fredon-Springdale Road, and turn left. Just over a mile down that you will find a parking lot to the Wildlife Management Area on your left. Other designated parking areas exist along Routes 208 and 611, with parking along the roads themselves not allowed. Parking for the Natural Area proper might be tried by driving another 0.3 miles to a junction, at which point you turn left and go for just under half a mile to a parking space on your left, which has a gate that shuts off a weedy road.

This road, says William J. Boyle, Jr., in his highly regarded book *A Guide to Bird Finding in New Jersey*, goes across a field with hedgerows and you take the right fork, the left going to the first parking lot. A three tenths of a mile walk brings you to the fence and gate of the Natural Area, which quickly becomes a woodland. On mossy boulders look for the unusual walking fern, with its solitary stretched triangular frond. You then enter a field and then another woods. Enter this and soon notice open water on your left downhill, Big Spring. With this variety of habitats surrounding you, field trips should be among the best ever taken.

Trout in the surrounding management area are stocked by the state Division of Fish, Game and Wildlife. In the uplands you will find grouse, woodcock, rabbits, squirrels, and deer. Various plantings, hedgerows, and cuttings have been arranged to enhance these species.

Sussex County
Hamburg Mountain Wildlife Management Area

On the north side of Route 23, north of Ogdensburg, a parking lot gives you access to this forested 2,442 acres of rough mountain hiking. Here is a chance to see wild turkeys while you are doing your best to maintain decent footing. From a distance during autumn, you may have the chance to follow long and broken waves of color that will convince you mountain hiking is just the thing to do.

Sussex County
High Point State Park
Dryden Kuser Natural Area

Follow Route 23 northward for its last 12 miles to just after its juncture with Route 519, and you will enter the southeastern edge of this 850-acre preserve. From the park office along 23 take either Kuser Road or the one-way Scenic Drive and then Monument Drive, which encircles the 220-foot tall High Point Monument (elevation: 1803 feet). Here you will be looking out southwest on the Delaware Water Gap of the Kittatinny Ridge, west on the Poconos, north on the Catskills and Shawangunks, and east on the New Jersey Highlands.

Perhaps most surprising is a northern bog at the 1500-foot elevation. Locally called the Cedar Swamp, it is the first Natural Area to be dedicated in the state, done so on October 12, 1965, to the late Senator Dryden and Colonel Kuser. This is the northern extreme habitat of southern white cedar, tall trees of which, along with rhododendrons, cloak the grounds here—quite far from the lands in southern New Jersey where you may have met them before. Northern waterthrushes nest in the tangles, helped by the mosses which are so common. Deer populations may be assumed to be about, even though they are not immediately visible, by the pruning they do while browsing during winters of starving on the banks of evergreen rhododendrons.

As with the rest of the park, overall about 14,000 acres in size, the rocks are sedimentary and of extreme age, going back to the Cambrian through Devonian (first fish) Periods. The ridges are of sandstone and conglomerate, the valleys of worn shale and limestone, making the park a fine geological part of the Appalachian Trail.

Sussex County
Stokes State Forest
Tillman Ravine Natural Area

These 500 or so acres of anticline sandstone and red shale rock formations with oaks, hemlocks, white pines and others are bounded on the north by Brinks Road and on the South by Woods Road. There are at least a mile of well-delineated footpaths and several rustic bridges among the songs of warblers and hermit thrushes. You will enjoy the bold rock outcrops and ledges down which Tillman Brook cascades in a vertical descent of more than 100 feet under hemlocks and rhododendrons. A Park Superintendent wrote some years ago, "The thermal drop that one experiences in summer upon entering the ravine, the fresh clean air, the tall swaying trees, the rhododendron in bloom, the early morning songs of the birds, the icicles in winter, the rays of sunlight on a misty day, all give the visitor a grateful feeling about being alive."

Naturalists who look for inhabitants of creeks will be pleased to note that there are not only crayfish and mayfly nymphs but plenty of brook trout white suckers, blacknose and longnose dace, and creek chub. When you reach the bottom of the ravine look for a circular-shaped smooth-walled cut in the creek floor. This is a pothole, called here the Teacup, which is a gouge made by sand and rock sent into a swirling spin by the running water, acting effectively much like the scouring of a pot.

To get here off Route 615, Walpack (Flatbrook) Road, turn east at Main (Tillman) Road just north of the National Park Service District Office on your right. You will immediately pass the Sandyston Township Town Hall on your left. Tillman eventually becomes Struble Road to the north and links up with Route 206, where if you turn right you will find the Stokes State Forest headquarters.

Sussex County
Swartswood Lake State Park

Just north of the center of Newton take Route 618 west off Rt. 206. Where it meets Rt. 94 turn left and then shortly go right on Rt. 610. Soon go right on Rt. 619, and you will quickly be entering Swartswood Lake State Park. To make the most of the fee, levied during summer, do your naturing around Duck Pond, on the right side of the road. Here is a romantic habitat of uplands sliding down, as it were, into a small natural lake. The times when waterfowl are migrating through may be your favorite, and *A Guide to Bird Finding in New Jersey* indicates you may well find scaup, bufflehead, and common goldeneye here along with an occasional oldsquaw and scoter. Another pleasure is the ring of frog choruses especially from around Duck Pond during April and May.

Sussex and (a little) Passaic Counties
Wawayanda State Park

Up in north-central New Jersey against the New York border of Sussex County, this is a great forested complex of many nature trails, which I can only hint of here. It can be reached by taking Route 94 north across the New York State border and then turning right on Wawayanda Road, which winds through the park. Along this road you will find the Park Office and a road to very nearby 255-acre Wawayanda Lake, with its four islands, where you can swim, fish, rent boats, look for ospreys, etc.

In the Park are also two areas designated by the State as Natural Areas. When going here I was advised to bring along, as in many natural places in north Jersey, both a snake bite kit and a portable CB radio. The first Natural Area, Wawayanda Hemlock Ravine, consists of about 400 acres of hemlocks together with oaks, hickories, and others. The scenic quality is outstanding. Wawayanda Creek here is steep with large boulders and shelf rocks with deep plunge pools, all under a dense cover of large hemlocks. To get here plan on walking for perhaps two miles. Fish you might expect here include largemouth bass, redbreast sunfish, chain and grass pickerel, white suckers, common shiners, creek chub, cutlips minnows, and tesselated darters.

The second, Wawayanda Swamp, is about 2,000 acres of northern swamp habitats (red and white cedar), northeastern forests (maple-ash, oak-hickory), and on the western side basically untouched 8.5-acre Laurel Pond, formed by glacial cutting and now fed by springs and an outlet stream from the lake. Part of the pond shoreline is interestingly lined by floating mat bog vegetation, while overhead you might expect to hear northern and Louisiana waterthrushes. Fish in the pond are pretty much the same species as in the lake: black crappies, bluegill sunfish, chain pickerel, creek chubsuckers, golden shiners, largemouth bass, redbreast and pumpkinseed sunfish, and yellow perch, with occasionally the bass and pickerel being notably large. In the lake five and six pound bass, trout, and northern pike turn up fairly often. One should not be surprised that the name Wawayanda came from Indian language "Wa-wa-anda" meaning "water on the mountain."

Bearfort Mountain shows Devonian rocks notably overlaid by scrub oaks and carrying glacially scooped Terrace Pond with its surrounding muff of rhododendrons.

224

Sussex and Warren Counties
Allamuchy State Park

Straddling Route 80 and lying west of Route 206 is this 7,000 or so acres of hardwood forest. The Ranger Station can be reached off the Waterloo-Willow Grove Road, which goes west from Route 206 just north of the Route 183 connection. Entrance to the Deer Lake Park Natural Area can be made from Deer Park Road going east from Route 517 on the western side of the Park. After the drive, you will have to walk about a mile to this lake.

Here is a giant forest spattered with the diversity given by a few fields and special groves, such as some with hemlocks. Much of the area will be known to few people, however, but *A Guide to Bird Finding in New Jersey* notes that wild turkeys are succeeding well here as well as winter wrens. The turkeys, he says, will perhaps be in evidence if you enter the park by going north on Route 517 from Exit 19 of Route I-80, travelling about 1.3 miles and taking a right on a dirt road, which will soon take you to the appropriate fields. At the end of that road, by the way, you can take a left on another dirt road, park, and walk on it uphill to a trail on the right that goes up to the top of Allamuchy Mountain itself. If you hike to the top, remember that you are doing an equivalent of travelling northward up the continent as vertical represents latitude—1,000 feet up in actual elevation equals a trip of about 600 miles north, a hundred feet of elevation equals about one day's change in season.

The 46 acres of Deer Park Pond, lay here in an open and fern-laden woods. It is fairly shallow, with a maximum depth of only 10 feet due to the gradual filling in of sediment, the south portion becoming choked with weeds during the summer. The north side has been mildly denuded of trees in the past from the activities of introduced beavers. You will see some of their lodges out in the pond. Osprey sometimes nest here, and a fair variety of fish do well also. Fishermen enjoy the hemlock and pine groves along the bank, and may catch fish such as largemouth bass, chain pickerel, yellow perch, bluegill and pumpkinseed sunfish, and black crappies.

Off Waterloo Road is the Saxton Falls parking lot, identified by a Morris Canal sign. Here is one nineteenth century lock of the 34 in a canal which, like so many, soon fell to trains. During its peak year of operating, though, 1866, the conduit carried nearly 900,000 tons of materials.

Warren County

Warren County
Frelinghuysen Township
Johnsonburg Natural Area

Here, on eleven acres just northwest of the crossing of the Erie Lackawanna Railroad and Dark Moon Road, is a cross-section of northern habitats, a site that even includes some rare plant species and some unusual geologic features. Dark Moon Road is the northern terminis of Allamuchy Road, Route 612, which farther south (as Johnsonburg Road) crosses Route 517 shortly after 517 goes north from Route I-80, where it can be reached at an Exit.

Warren County
Hope Township
Bursch Sugar Maple Natural Area

Touching the east side of Honeywell Road, terminating at Delaware Road to the south and Knowlton Delaware Road to the north, this 25-acre sugar maple forest shows what a climax forest of the northeastern states looks like. See Osmun Forest Natural Area.

Warren County
Knowlton Township
Osmun Forest Natural Area

Lying inside the corner formed where Knowlton Delaware Road is joined by Honeywell Road from the south, this ten-acre hardwood forest shows the gradual succession leading to a typical northeastern mixed growth of hardwoods. See Bursch Sugar Maple Natural Area.

Warren County
Worthington State Forest

Take Interstate 80 west and at the last exit, Exit 1, go right into this deep dark forest of 5,830 acres. You are now on Old Mine Road or River Road, one of the earliest roads around. The State office is about four miles ahead, on your left, as is a campground. Farther along, and out in the Delaware River, is well-known Tocks Island, part of this preserve.

You can get to the Dunnfield Creek Natural Area, about 100 acres in extent, by various trails off Old Mine Road or from one trail leaving Route 80 at a parking lot on the east side less than a mile before Exit 1. Here sugar and striped maples, hemlocks, tulip trees, black birches, white ashes and black oaks dominate, with a strong understory of rhododendrons, giving the land an aspect of the hemlock-hardwoods forests so familiar across New England. Among the hemlocks and spruces look for northern finches during winter. When spring comes, you will also enjoy the sprays of white and pink mountain laurel blossoms.

Brown and rainbow trout, both introduced, are doing well, as are native brook trout and pickerel frogs. You will also find most of the mammals you might expect, from deer to tree-climbing gray foxes. And over 40 species of birds have been recorded as common or better. Come as spring warms the mountains to be in on the peenting calls and aerial displays of male woodcocks.

Off the same departure point from Route 80, you can take the Appalachian Trail to forty-one acre Sunfish Pond, a small lake that is pleasant for its clear water, lacking as it is in excessive natural fertility. The fish present are those historically naturally occurring there, and so you will find brown bullheads, chain pickerels, pumpkinseed sunfish, and yellow perch. They are not the only hunters of insects around, of course, and their very success implies that you can sit along the shore and watch dragonflies and swifts dart over the water. Dragonflies, incidentally, are known to establish feeding and sexual territories.

The Appalachian Trail overall is about 2000 miles (3,218 km.) long. It reaches from Mt. Springer, Georgia, to Mt. Katahdin, Maine, and crosses the Delaware River from Pennsylvania just north of the Delaware Water Gap. It then ascends the mountain ridge and eventually goes northeast into Stokes State Forest and High Point State Park.

236

Photographs

A shaded summer stroll at the Rancocas Nature Center in Burlington County (pg. 28) can reveal an abundance of wildlife and a variety of fields, woods, and wetlands. (Photograph by Deborah Hogan.)

A visit to the top of the summit in Tourne Park (Booton and Denville Townships, Morris County, pg. 144) provides a spectacular view of the surrounding area, including the New York City Skyline. (Photograph by Thomas Hogan.)

The boulder-strewn gorge of Trout Creek in Hacklebarney State Park, Morris County (pg. 152) is a beautiful place to visit in every season. Summer can be especially nice, however, as mixed hardwoods such as oaks and maples provide shade down near the running waters. (Photograph by Thomas Hogan.)

241

Forsythe National Wildlife Refuge in Atlantic County (pg. 8) offers possibly the best birding in the state. Some of the most magnificent times come as thousands of flocked snow geese glide in during October and November. (Photograph by Millard Davis.)

Island Beach State Park in Ocean County (pg. 168) is a ten-mile-long barrier beach that remains fairly undisturbed. The mists and fine salt spray of some mornings might make you think of the first people to land here, unaware of the gigantic continent ahead. (Photograph by Millard Davis.)

Hawks and other birds of prey are prevalent throughout New Jersey, from the mountains of the North to the Pine Barrens of the South. This photograph of a recently-hatched hawk was taken somewhere in between, in the Morris, Harding, and Mendham area of Morris County (pg. 140). (Photograph by Millard Davis.)

Lebanon State Forest comprises about 22,216 acres in Burlington and Ocean Counties (pg. 32) Here you will find two ponds, Pakin and Deep Hollow, numerous streams, and a number of working and abandoned cranberry bogs. (Photograph by Thomas Hogan.)

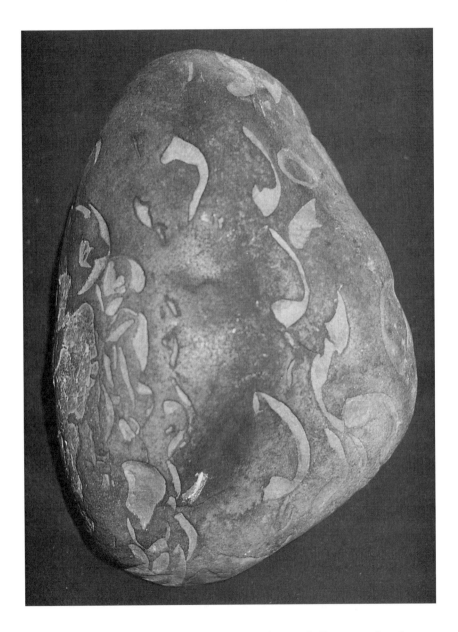

This stone, marked with signs carved by the Delaware Indians, was found some-where along the Delaware River in North Central New Jersey. (Photograph by Millard Davis.)

Part 2 - The Puzzle Joined

Have you ever wished to bring together a whole of nature that was once but a collection of parts? To see unity in the seemingly disparate, the musical score, as it were, that was once but notes?

To dip your fingers in water that is quiet with yellow pond lilies, gone turbulent with the rush of wood ducks? To freeze an irresolute deer, look down on the slick pate of a tall great blue heron? Even perhaps to pull aside and stop of an evening and let the mood of the season overtake you, that you be swallowed up in the whole, immersed where once you only floated.

At least two such voyages are available in New Jersey to you, the Sindbad of nature in its various forms. And both are easily arrived at. The first is often cited as a family event, commonly used as a Boy or Girl Scout trip. The second many of you have taken commonly. The first is a canoe trip through a part of the famous New Jersey Pine Barrens. The second is a vehicle ride south and north on the New Jersey Garden State Parkway.

In the following pages you will be invited to visualize this world as I, and certainly many others, have found such adventures. To enter a dim outdoors, here gradually lightening first with silhouettes and then with almost tangible substance, the substance to be made real by your own eventual traveling.

NOT SO BARREN A PATH

You have to like the metaphor of "The Pine Barrens." It implies that nothing is there. Well, I have eaten well in the Barrens at nature's expense (partially by beating squirrels to chestnut oak acorns), listened to choruses under the moonlight (frogs calling from trees and waters), and sped a canoe faster under branches than ever I plan to do again (during one floodtime the bough of a white cedar even flipped a friend overboard). So, I come here for adventure.

On the seventeenth of June one spring, a season that arrives a little later for plants in the wetland part of the Barrens because of the cooling effect of the water, I pressed aside typically stocky boughs of Atlantic white cedars and entered a swamp that was just coming into full bloom. Sweet fragrance of swamp azalea hung along the spongy shore. I could see from the long tubular blossoms why azaleas had for years been thought to be a kind of honeysuckle. Actually the latter are even in another family, the Caprifoliaceae, one of those few groups of plants whose members have opposite leaves—the leaves arise in pairs, those of a pair being opposite each other on the stem. Azaleas, on the other hand, belong to the family Ericaceae. Like rhododendron, mountain laurel, leatherleaf, cranberry, and others of the family, these shrubs prefer acid soils. And so acid are the Barrens soils in general that they are not only high in such plants but low in earthworms! Possibly it is not only acids that restrict the worms. A number of plants, such as the staggerbush which was on that day shaking its white, bell blossoms as I passed—produce poisons which can not only stagger but knock down cattle.

Only a film of water identified this flat land as a swamp. Small yellow flowers of bladderwort pointed up deeper places. Here the purse-like bladders on the roots snapped open to suck in minute insects and crustaceans such as cyclops and daphnia, or water fleas. Sometimes the water surface had been blotted out by enough scum from iron salts to make it nearly opaque, difficult to judge for depth. To be really sure of footing you had to take a route that led across white pebbles. These were not made of marl, as has so often been claimed. Marl in this area was created more than 65 million years ago during

249

the Cretaceous Period and was laid down underneath or outside the visible Pine Barrens land. Being alkaline, it supports earthworms and would fit few of these cedar swamp plants. Most of this surface land comes from Quaternary Period sources, our period, and so is of relatively recent origin. I was choosing pebbles and hard-packed sand to cross. The darker sand, more oiled by organic debris, sank like a trap.

Deeper in the ground strata, marl or "greensands" *do* support the Barrens. And in them lies water-soluble iron. When the underground water, saturated with organic ooze, flows through this marl, the marl attracts the iron, which it eventually heaves to the surface. We see it, now oxidized, as a golden sludge that loads down filamentous algae. The banks and beds of streams and bogs become coated with a hard ore. In the past these surface veins were mined for the product, which became known as "bog iron." It proved to be a weak industry, however. That iron took so long to build up that it could be mined only once every 20 years!

Except for that organic ooze which I habitually avoided stepping on, however, no one would ever have thought of this skim of a swamp or bog as being depressing or forbidding in the way that untramped wetlands have often been pictured. Actually the swamp remains in my mind as a land of orchids. Here stood sprays of grass pinks, each a stalk with but a single leaf and topped by a crest of magenta-pink blossoms. Snake mouth blooms, in tones of white and pink, each stuck out a fringed tongue, useful to insects which attempt to land on the flower. Botanists have treated this shape as being a lip with hair, and so the second part of the scientific name of *Pogonia ophioglossoides* means bearded. Bumblebees fit naturally into its curves, just as they do into those of the splotched magenta blossom of cedar bog arethusa which also lives here. Both flowers not only offer but actually pour pollen onto the departing bee's head in nature's scheme to fertilize the next of these flowers visited.

Natural plant groupings stood out. On one tuft of muck clung a single rose pogonia or snake mouth, a yellow bog asphodel, a six-inch-tall Atlantic white cedar, and several wiry thread-leaved sundews. In several places, like survivors of an antiquated buddy system, little curly grass fern and Carolina club moss stood side by side. There, soaring to a few inches above the coiled springs of the sterile fronds, fertile stalks of the fern lifted up their minute spore cases that so closely resemble toothbrushes.

A third grouping of cedar bog plants came more to my mind than eye, namely the oddities. Here were mop-like blossoms of orange milkwort, which you have to come to the Barrens to see. Like all milkworts, these are pollinated primarily by bees. Then there was bog aster, unusual in that it blossoms during spring. Very wooly gold cress reminded me of two other furry inhabitants of harsh windy places—dusty miller of our sandy seashores and lead plant of mid-

250

western prairies. Yellow-blossomed bog asphodel, which was first described for the world from Pine Barrens specimens, reaches its northern limits here, as do many plants. For all that, a toad, Fowler's toad, is itself virtually replaced by the American toad north of Trenton, New Jersey, just a quick drive above the Barrens. Finally, among the plant curiosities here, golden club, which has horizontally spread-eagled leaves that shed water, stood out like green stars here and there. Many of the leaf blades still balanced drops of rain from an early morning shower. The drops had been balled up into extra-large jewels.

Where such cedar bogs deepen into lakes, snow geese roam in, often by the hundreds during autumn as they head down the coast for wintering grounds between here and North Carolina. Sometimes they make a gigantic nonstop flight that carries them 1,600 miles, from James Bay in Canada to the Gulf Coast in Louisiana. Sunlight striking their feathers can make a flock that is more than a mile away appear as a flashing streamer, one that may be made up of nearly a thousand birds. When several thousand descend on a phragmites marsh, even those tall bony reeds may be stomped flat over hundreds of square yards. During spring they again return, heading for their summer breeding grounds in the Arctic. From here their next leap may be so great that they span New England with hardly a rest. And their voices, thousands strong coming down through the night, say "We are here, and going."

Their counterparts, the whistling swans, fly so high that even their doubled or tripled whistle may be missed. They leave not so often from trampled land but from ruffled water where they have been poking down for roots and stems. I see them in lesser numbers so that their half dozen skips on the water show up all through the take-off. Old cranberry bog lakes hold scattered flocks which I pick up one by one walking through the Barrens.

It was only a half hour into one evening after watching such scaling flights of whistlers that I saw my first Pine Barrens sunset. A loose string of clouds stretched in undulating threads across the horizon like an immutable migrating flock of the birds. I then noticed in almost contacting parallel another such "flight," the reflections of those clouds across acres of cedar water.

By way of contrast, traveling down one of the Pine Barrens streams like the Mullica River or Oswego Creek brings you face to face with a swiftly changing slice through several different wildlife and forest types. Sometimes you can *hear* the difference. Pine warblers, often facing down while chipping at insects under the pitch pine bark, are seasonally so evident that their trilling has been termed "The Song of the Pine Barrens." Listen for notes which mount the chromatic scale to separate out a companion, the prairie warbler. It is not, incidentally, a bird of the prairies but of young forests. Most breed in openings, often where the Barrens are brushy with not only low trees but switch grasses and broomsedges.

251

During one canoe trip we were relatively inundated with bird songs over a brief straight stretch of the winding Oswego Creek. Within only a few seconds we heard redstarts, white-throated sparrows, rufous-sided towhees, white-breasted nuthatches, yellowthroats, and Carolina wrens—and we saw a turkey vulture. So gentle is the usual pace of this stream that it is no surprise to drift down past schools of whirligig beetles that are swimming upstream.

One moment you sail under pines and oaks, another beneath the white undersides of swamp magnolia and the scarlet autumn blaze of black-gum leaves. Then the columnar spires of Atlantic white cedar.

A low understory of mountain laurel is likely to parallel almost all of your narrow defile. Along with it come moments during many weeks of midsummer when the long narrow clusters of the white flowers of sweet pepperbush shake nearby. The single pigtail of each fruit makes these shrubs easy to identify while on trips during winter. Blueberries can hardly be missed. They form a wiry hardwood stand beneath even such low woodland layers as leatherleaf and sheep laurel, or lamb's kill.

Late summer is the right time for mixed colors here. Bloodred leaves of huckleberry, best separated from blueberry by the glisten of resin on its leaves, point upward beneath powdery white cedar cones. Over among nearly barren gravels bog asphodel sends up its spartan stalk that terminates as a spike of tiny massed orange blossoms. Each flower of meadow beauty, *Rhexia virginica*, spreads four broad magenta petals behind a spidery tangle of projecting golden anthers. Alive or fading, these half-clenched male parts remind me of the autumn flowers of witch hazel. Finally, some travelers are lucky enough to see along marshy sides the pink St. Johnswort *Triadenum virgininum*—it is only local St. Johnswort so colored.

Where such streams expand into semi-marshes, the white candy-like heads of pipewort poke out of the water on rod-like stems that are devoid of foliage. Down at their bases, several feet deep, spread out the elongate sharp leaves. About it are often scattered the pancake leaves of water shield, gelatinous to the touch. Here and there around the country the leaves, stems, and roots of water shield are eaten in a salad, but I do not find the plant listed in such a standard work as Euell Gibbons' *Stalking The Wild Asparagus*. Fragrant water lilies are not mentioned either. Their tubers, like the rootstocks of water shield, are nutritious with starch and can be treated like potatoes. No need to feel wasteful of nature's bounty here if you skip these items—local mammals and birds will be just as pleased. To catch the water lily blossoms most full open, come on a bright summer day between seven in the morning and one in the afternoon, for they are just opening or closing before and after that period. I also find them partially shut during the day if clouds cover as much as 60 to 70 percent of the sky.

While many people miss the cedar swamps and streams as they pass through the Barrens, no one fails to notice the forests of ragged pines so far inland. If you are coming from the seashore, they at first seem but an extension of low coastal growth. Soon, however, the forest asserts itself by towering over almost all else. The ability of the pines to sprout again after a forest fire has given them at least temporary dominance in many parts of the Pine Barrens. In others the many oaks rule, while elsewhere they split the land fifty-fifty.

One autumn I began naming some oaks of the Pine Barrens by their interesting varieties of leaves. (I was taking a relatively dangerous route, tackling an art which is often best left to comparing acorns—but these may be missing where gray squirrels have been particularly active). The gracefully embayed leaves of the holly leaf oak with their needle-tipped lobes illustrate why they are so named. Post oak took its name from the fence posts it became so readily in the hands of pioneers, but for the origin of *Stellata*, from post oak's scientific name of *Quercus* (oaks) *stellata*, I could easily look to the leaves: those of post oak are shaped somewhat like stars. Leaves of a blackjack oak, though, might come in two distinctively different forms. Fortunately both always suggest to me the broad boat-shape of certain old-time blackjacks or "saps." Black oak I picked out for its lobes which expand near the tips; those of similar red oak narrow down. Chestnut oak leaves are easy for anyone to recognize from their sharply wavy margins; once I even discovered two American chestnut saplings while looking closely for the chestnut oaks which had been showering a particular path with mahogany- and butter-colored acorns. During one extended episode a migrating swarm of grasshoppers called the "post oak locust" made a kind of history among chestnut oaks here as the insects moved through the Lebanon State Forest tract of the Barrens. The overwhelming mass left its most permanent known record there by destroying not post but chestnut oaks while marching along at the rate of about one tenth of a mile each year.

Oak-pine forests are likely to be the most impressive of the piney woods, rising up to 50 feet or so. A mixture of oaks lives here with some having favorite stands. Black oak you can find in many stands, but to be sure you have it try peeling off some bark along a twig—the inner lining will be yellow to orange. This pigment once made a powerful dye, but it also had to be leached out by a tanner before he tried to use the tree's tannin for curing leather. Chestnut and white oak may rule another territory and scarlet oak yet a third. Thus these forests exist as patchworks, a hardwood quilt held together by pitch pines.

Blackjack oaks and pitch pines dominate most of the areas where the most extensive studies have been done to date. These are stocky forests, with the pines reaching up 25 feet and the oaks getting only 10 to 15 feet tall. Here is some of the best lowbush-blueberry and black-huckleberry picking around—

though I prefer collecting my blueberries along a cedar lake shore as I drift along in a canoe.

Possibly the best places to visualize how pitch pine fits in and has done so well in the face of competition with oaks is in the pitch pine lowlands, where pitch pine is almost the only tree. Here you can often see sand of the Lakewood series, with white grains across the surface and brown ones below. The water table lies only three feet below at the most. In such ground people need to use sewerage pipes, septic tanks being almost impossible. On most of these pitch pine landscapes young pines are not even around. The reason is that their seeds cannot break through the litter of needles and block of bark. The inference here is that they can germinate only on bare ground, which is exposed only by fire. In the lowlands it is easy to count the rings of "whorls" of pine branches all the way to the top and so estimate accurately the year of the last major fire. When tall oaks do occur with the pines, here you can guess that the land was protected against fire.

Ponds and sedgy-grassy marshes which are scattered about here make such areas places which you walk through with care. The curious spongs, pronounced "spungs" like "rungs," are pitch pine lowlands where the grayish, drooping-leaved low shrub called leatherleaf dominates. Dead leaves in the crown indicate that they have just passed through a harsh, killing winter. Ponds and streams here may be half-covered by savannas of leather-leaf and other shrubs.

During spring some people come to the Barrens just to collect the freshly emerged bracken ferns. While the later fronds are poisonous and have made these umbrella-like ferns an anathema to farmers with livestock, the fiddleheads of youth are delicious, whether eaten right on the spot or prepared like asparagus. These are one of the first plants to sprout up after a fire. And while the ground is clean you can easily see how common are white-tailed deer here by checking for their tracks in the clearings.

You don't have to look far for animal evidence in the Pygmy Forest, the Plains. Here, in a land of four- to six-foot-tall pitch pines and blackjack and scrub oaks, pine cones that have been gnawed down look as large as Christmas ornaments as they indicate the presence of red squirrels. Break open a gray dead tree trunk only an inch or so in diameter, and out pour termites. Deer prints hold the sand for a while, out in a dwarf land where much of the understory consists of such shoe-level plants as reindeer lichen, *Hudsonia*, pyxie moss, bearberry, and broom crowberry.

How strange this forest is becomes even more clear when you realize that pyxie moss only looks like a moss. Actually the dense mats are of a flowering plant. I have seen it during spring when the white flowers on the minute green leaves reminded me of artistically knitted flowers sewn onto a hand-knit blanket. At that time of the year pyxie was paralleling in the Pygmy Forest what bloodroot, spring beauty, and others were doing in hardwood forests not too far away. During summer the leaves turn reddish, then bronze in autumn, like various oak leaves of the taller Barrens forests.

While pyxie moss is a southerner, reaching up the Atlantic coastline in isolated spots from South Carolina, a near relative is an alpine type, occupying cold mountain summits. Both have found success in lands of little competition. So also has the flat tangle of woody stems called broom-crowberry. Essentially this shrub may be a relic, left over from the glaciers and now living in a kind of safety at the southern end of its coastal plain range.

Like these, many good things end in the Pine Barrens. I have a prized photograph of one of the butterflies, the red spotted purple; even though spending its summer on the wing, this lively butterfly which loves the refuse along shady roads, travels almost no farther along the coast south. And the golden red variegated fritillary suspends its northward ascent up the coast here. Leaf-cutting ants terminate their building of new crescent-shaped nests pretty much within the Barrens borders as far as New Jersey is concerned. Anderson's tree frog occurs but sparingly outside these cedar swamps, and almost invariably in such habitats.

Hopefully, with care for these remarkable forests and wetlands, this sort of ending will be the only sort. And we may even have one or two beginnings, such as that of Hessel's hair-streak. For forty years before its discovery, no new butterfly had been seen in the northeastern part of the United States. If the Pine Barrens itself is a holdover from glacial times, as some authorities believe, or even if we view it merely as the remarkably untouched community it still is, who knows what further secrets it holds? And which we must protect.

255

CORRIDOR THROUGH WILDLIFE

In the green hall I did not pause. Sometimes I hurried in darkness, other times in columns of light. Now I rushed in shadows of trees, again I balanced as on a fine black thread cutting sunlit meadows.

To the west along this smoothest of highway openings reached far woods. To the east they went out to sea.

Suddenly I swept up a rise, and all about me white birds swirled as though motes of vapor were being blown from a boiling caldron below. In actuality, though, this was a drive down the state of New Jersey, and this part was merely a lift up and over a river, which here flattened out into an estuary of the Atlantic Ocean; while driving the arching bridge I could see where shining gulls were scaling up from salt marsh grasses that spread out beside the widening river. Perhaps speeding motorists had kept them always on alert for bits of bread and similar treasures they could catch on the wing. Then I dropped again into the blinking green slats of a corridor through trees and shrubs and weeds. Butterflies leapt among flowers, their wings opening and closing like colorful books being read by unseen eyes. Birds sang in single notes—I slowed down to catch whole phrases.

So it was that I was driving through a part of the southbound lane of the appropriately named Garden State Parkway (or GSP), and it was a corridor through wildlife.

How many times I had driven this route and had missed the point I do not care to consider. But never again. And in fact as quickly as possible I took out my camera and began recording some favorite scenes—especially those where the highway shoulder might be widened to accept more parked vehicles, without intruding on the wildness.

Where are these best lookouts? Well, imagine beginning at the juncture of east-west Route 195 and the south-running lane of the Garden State Parkway. This meeting also approximates your departing from the geology and ecology of the slender Inner Coastal Plain to the inhabitants and sandier soils of the broad Outer Coastal Plain, which makes up all of our seashore and most of the New Jersey Pine Barrens.

Both lands are sandy enough, however, to walk there and recall the ancient ocean which once washed these grounds. Driving from one to the other, over an imaginary line, you can often point out the shift in forest from oak to oak-pine and then to pine-oak, the last being typical of the wooded shoreline.

I use the Parkway mile markers here to establish specific sites, and it is especially pleasing that the distances are broken down further into tenths of a mile. It is, of course, a travel that should be renewed, say, every 10 or 15 years, to keep up with changes. For instance about 15 years ago I noted between markers 95.9 and 95.8, which stand about that far from the southern terminus of the GSP, a deep chasm of a smooth-flowing creek cutting a gap through a sleeve of woods to the west, splitting the wooden median on my right, slipping under the northbound lane, and departing to the Atlantic Ocean. Today, 1996, the slash is closed over, though attractively.

But it nevertheless remains for us a beginning. From here on you are in a corridor through changing scenes of wildlife. Even during the earliest days of spring, when snow has left and there are no tracks, the barest trees at your sides become perches for birds of the roadside, every stump potentially a springboard for chickadees. It is a matter of hours until the old fallen oak leaves rustle with passing frogs on their way toward calling from trunk and limb.

At marker 93.2 you meet the exit for Route 549 to Lakewood and Brick Township, while just after 89.8 you can join Route 70—useful designations to the follower of nature, who can hereby also drop in to pick up specific targets along the GSP.

Just south of 86.0 trumpet vines blossomed this past summer. And at 84.7 you help maintain these views, at the Toms River Toll Plaza. If you haven't already, you will come to feel that you owe more, for this window onto nature.

And it is truly a window, that first golden opening onto other broad vistas as you drive up on marker 81.4, just after passing the exit to Route 37 at 82.5 and the Toms River/Lakehurst exit at 81.8.

By easing up, you can catch the rough break in shrubs and trees which occurs to the west between 81.4 and 81.3. Here you suddenly look down on a totally different land. Perched as it were in a front row balcony seat, you are at the brim of a panorama of tens of acres of freshwater marsh, a land of maybe snowy egrets rimmed by forest. With binoculars or telescope you yourself enter that world. I have arrived here when the surface of the marsh was a pincushion of weedy stubs and Canada geese were upending like corks in the cold water of spring. On another occasion gulls were flapping up like white sheets in vagrant winds. And I have paused longer when the purple spires of thousands of pickerel weeds made this garden at the mouth of Wrangel Brook seem a dark reflection of the summer sky. Inured today to the slashing roar of passing automobiles and trucks, deer might be seen nosing through tangles at marsh edge, pickerel fish bending among submerged stems, black swallowtail butterflies shifting from blossom to blossom like bits of agitated paper. Overall, the great marsh seems like a crowded wet prairie.

Garden State Parkway authorities evidently have also seen the potential for a semi-preserve here, for down at marker 80.4, four-tenths of a mile south of the exit to Routes 530 and 9, you meet a sign which indicates deer territory. Then just before marker 79, appropriately in a jacket of pines and oaks, you are welcomed to the Pinelands National Reserve, where the long promise of saving has begun to be fulfilled.

It is a sign that you are entering the amphitheatre of an idea. Here you may find forests wired off by ripping strands of catbrier, vines with thorns that wordlessly say "No Trespassing." Or you may parallel a graded series of plants that rise westward from roadside grasses and weeds through low shrubbery to a horizon of trees. In grassy openings you may find tromped down runs of deer that lead to shelter, clusters of tightly woven myrtle shrubs (the berries of which once supplied settlers with wax, now are important perhaps primarily as fuel to migrating birds). Birds of the open field such as goldfinches and bobolinks sing on the wing, while only a few hundred yards away owls seem to have been poked down among the high shaggy heads of pines.

And so much is close enough to pick up the breezes of passing vehicular traffic.

Stopping in the Food & Fuel depot at marker 76.3 need not be but a civilization trap: the entry is lined on your left with ferns. During summer the dominant fern of Pine Barrens dry woodlands, bracken, seems shrubby, becomes almost indistinguishable from the woody low blue berries; early in spring its knobby heads were probably edible, though they soon became poisonous; September finds them bronzing in color and curling into viney knots. Autumn will begin to close with frosts which kill the flat leafy fronds of sensitive fern, on this stop also.

At 75.6 you find the Forked River/Waretown exit.

Tall trees come right down to creek's edge where the narrow Middle Branch of Forked River crosses through an evergreen cover of Atlantic white cedars to pass under the Parkway at marker 73. Here dark waters reflect cleanly as though designed as a mirror to blue sky and surrounding green flame. A similar view occurs at 71.9, only this time you can look both west and east, up and down the South Branch. It will be one of the few occasions when you can see through the usual eastside banks of trees—the northbound lane is but a light stroke across the woods over there.

Half a mile farther and you can pull into the Oyster Creek Picnic Area. Sunlight filters through pitch pines, so noticeable for the tufts of needles scattered up their trunks, curve-thorned catbrier vines wire a few paths closed, and this is in many ways Pine Barrens country up close. Usually a secluded place

259

to park can be found, and your car becomes a blind inside a living birdhouse. They arrive first as sounds, then as silhouettes flickering among branches. On occasions in such a place I have noticed on a dead tree the smooth hole leading to a flicker's nest. Perhaps the same pair of birds has dived into this retreat year after year, since they mate for life and will even return year after year—this also reduces the amount of drilling they will have to do with their somewhat curved bills. Anyway, among such surroundings, I often settle for a sandwich and coke.

A slick palisade of the Atlantic white cedars, known to travelers in the Pine Barrens for the graceful spires which guard the waterways and indicate dark drying swamps, closely guides the path, golden brown from tannins of cedars and oaks, of Oyster Creek at 71.0. True to its best conditions of growth, this stand simply excludes humans by being so tightly woven—except I sometimes wonder what it would be like on a winter day to ride a sled up one of the iced over rivulets that poke out from under the ground-skimming branches.

Between 69.8 and 69.6 you glide past a vale of pines and oaks, and your relative height puts you actually within their canopy. At 68.9 you halt and give your due at the Barnegat Plaza, while at 68.0 you can exit on Route 554 to Barnegat and Chatsworth, and at 64.2 you can contact Route 72.

The exit at marker 59.0 brings you to Route 539. At exit 57.4 Mill Branch Creek, thickly cloaked with trees, winds through water plants on its way farther south to Bass River.

Some cash or a token of your affection is due at 53.7, the New Gretna Plaza. Half a mile farther you can depart to New Gretna/Batsto Village.

Now you enter the great plains of this adventure as suddenly the yellow tide of salt marshes rushes out before you where the Bass River stretches wide just after 52.0. If gulls drifting at raceway speed over the Parkway sent your thoughts skyward, if a seaside odor turned the day around, or even if only the reading of a map promised it, any reason at all is enough to ease up here, drive more slowly, and think of this horizon which does lie eastward beyond the edge of the continent.

But, if you must miss this one, be ready for another to the east a mile and a half farther on, the Mullica River marshland beginning at 50.5. Such wetlands are reckoned as one of the richest of all life zones, the vegetation being a bank of protein because such acres can produce more than five times as many tons of plant substance as wheat plains.

With strong binoculars you can probably see to the right at 49.7 black ribbed mussels huddled in clusters among cordgrass roots which have been exposed at low tide. In only an hour one of these shellfish, an ingredient of poultry food, will when submerged pass more than a gallon of water through its system. All too often, though, that liquid has been polluted by the very habitat which the mussel prefers, so we tend to skip it as food.

With this world of marshes, you are following part of the huge Atlantic flyway, the route that millions of birds will take south in autumn...and return on the following spring. At every opening now wet plains will take you to far horizons. And you are stopping as the birds have for millions of years, which has made this coastline one of the great preserves of all time.

At 48.3 you can depart for Route 9, or at 44.3 leave for Pomona.

But, for another sort of break, at 41.6 is the Atlantic City Service Area, where can be seen a light stand of grey birch. Able to withstand soils low in nutrients, this is the birch species of upland woods in the Pine Barrens. Also notice in season around the main building the many house sparrows, especially recognizable by the black throat patch of the male, while the female and young have undersides that have the tone of a dark cloud. In less than a century now, the species, introduced to North America as a few birds let loose in Central Park, New York City, in 1850, has swept over the temperate United States from the Atlantic to the Pacific. If you yourself have grown tired of the insistent chirping, think of the farmers whose fields they rape of grain.

Guests such as these often leap into great prominence. For example the starling, similarly freed in Central Park, only in 1890, and the gypsy moth, escaped in Medford, Massachusetts, about 1868-1869. None had competitors or enemies of any significance over here. On the other hand, probably insects have never successfully invaded the ocean because too many foes await them there.

At 46.1 you will see Atlantic white cedars on both sides of the GSP, implying a wetland embracing this corridor through wildlife.

At 44.2 notice the open understory; here as in similar places the ground cover is likely to be thick with small blueberry shrubs.

Route 30 is met at 40.0 , the Atlantic City Expressway at 37.2, and Routes 322 and 40 intersect at 36.8, with Route 563 arriving at 36.1. A small personal creek crosses just before 35.0

At 34.1 and 31.3 you can see to the west a line of red cedars. Nearly identical in size and therefore probably of the same age (even-aged), they may well have been planted as a barrier. If they were less uniform in size, they might have indicated an old fence, these trees then being the products of seeds dropped by birds that had perched there.

Golden flat marshes of Patcong Creek, flowing southeastward to Great Egg Harbor Bay, stand out at 31.1 for their expanses of short salt hay grass. Like freshly brushed hair, it lies flat and almost unnaturally smooth. When first I saw a meadow like this, I surmised someone had mowed it...not a bad image since centuries ago such plains were favorite pastures of cattle, and they are still cut over for fodder in haying drives.

Marker 30.4 finds a salt channel sliding beneath the highway, edging the north side of Exit 30, which sends you to Ocean City, Somers Point, and Route 9.

Any doubt that the territory here is tidal, with the water ebbing and flowing as the tides beat, disappears as one catches the channels between 29.8 and 29.7, as well as earlier at 30.4, during different cycles. At high tide you encounter a sluggish river; at low, grassy banks threaten to slump into this winding gouge through mud. Inch-wide holes in the weedless walls may tell where fiddler crabs burrow. They can control the fluids inside their bodies so as to ride out the changes from fresh to salt water here. But their young are a weak link: the eggs must be sent off in tidal currents, hopefully to find marshlands where the minute new crabs can dig in. It is an old system on earth—one way or another, every species, every individual, has its cave.

A fine view of the power plant at Somers Point of Great Egg Harbor Bay appears through fortress-like strands of Phragmites reeds between 29.2 and 29.1. (An overview had appeared from the bridge between 29.4 and 29.3, but that is a dangerous place to slow down.) Such immense stalks have been used for thatching buildings throughout the length of our coasts. Places like the imitatively restored colony at Jamestown, Virginia, show what tough structures they can be made into, that resilient walls and roofs were merely lashed bundles of reeds. In the hands of old masters, drawing pens shaped from these bone-like stems could stroke very fine art.

Another view, now from a road shoulder and at river level, opens shortly after the Great Egg Toll Plaza around 28.8.

And as for Phragmites, do not miss some of the smaller places. For instance at 26.3, just before the exit to Ocean City at 25.7, and at 25.0 small patches might become early each spring a home to redwinged blackbirds. During winter you might notice the reeds for their massed light golden heads.

Then, about just over a mile and a half farther south I have mentally set aide a valley, which we look down on from a bridge, as a bird sanctuary. An open marsh that is rimmed by grasses and guarded by forest, it appears to have no entry except this hole in the sky. Birds as uncommon as glossy ibises seem to fly here without noticing me. Black-and-white laughing gulls simply drop in from above, suggesting fine-pointed brushes dipping to stroke a final touch. On one summer morning I was reminded of the insects which spawn there as three great green darner dragonflies patrolled unhurriedly near me, skimming back and forth over the GSP road guard. And so, looming perhaps two hundred yards away on their eastern horizon, I never feel like an intruder.

Marker 22.9 brings the John R. Townshend/Shoemaker Holly Picnic Area, which is graced by tall holly trees.

At marker 21.0 a pond is being invaded by surrounding growth, but you might find wading birds. On one visit I spooked at least seven great blue herons. Breaking their stillness from among the beams of overhanging trees, their sharp cries of "kreik" seemed to come from deep rooms. Launching one at a time from darkness, they scaled individual routes over the green walls, suggesting personally held reticence to depart.

Then at 19.5 appears the Cape May Toll Plaza.

The Seaville Service Area with the Cape May Information room is available at 18.5.

A sign between 18.3 and 18.2 indicates you are now in the Belleplain State Forest. Sea Isle City and Woodbine are listed for the exit at 17.5.

Wide channels follow closely in the marshlands from 17.4 through 17.2. Here you may have a feeling of sitting right on top of this expanse, looking in a bay window as it were. This is low country, laced with wetlands. And so it is that all through these flats the red buds and flowers of water-loving red maple trees early in spring tell of acres of mud country which you cannot see from the GSP.

In a channel at 17.1 stood two men on a day in early March with a long, arc-ing seine that spanned the water between them. They said they were netting eels, each about two inches long. Their accents suggested Massachusetts, reminding one of the trouble the fishing industry up along the New England coast is having with Russian fishermen, who come over in what are essentially floating factories. These elvers, or young eels, had probably been spawned off Bermuda and had dropped out of the Gulf Stream near here. Eels are considered a favorite fish food, the commercial fishing industry stretching from the St. Lawrence River to at least Chesapeake Bay. The related European eel exits on the other side of the Atlantic Ocean.

You can leave for Swainton and Avalon on Route 9 just after 13.9.

Exits 10A and 10B for Cape May Court House and Stone Harbor occur just after marker 10.0, Route 657, the route east (via 10B) taking you past the Performing Arts Center, and then the research and educational property and building—gray gothic with a cupola and encircling widow's walk—of the Wetlands Institute. Beyond is Stone Harbor and further bird watching.

At 8.4 you can take Exit 9 to Route 9. Exit 4 at 8.4 puts you onto Route 47.

I have paused to photograph trumpet creeper vines in blossom at 4.2. The aerial rootlets they use for climbing enable them to coat shrubbery completely, and here as elsewhere along the Parkway they can lie as a monstrous spangled green blanket.

At 3.0 you will see a large pond to your left.

Two men netting elvers (eels) along the Garden State Parkway.

I once called and asked people who were canoeing down the channel between 2.5 and 2.4 what they were doing. The answer: crabbing.

A small stream slides under the GSP at 1.8.

I close my south-seeking notebook at 0.5, where the channel surges in a giant curve and leaves a flat muck bar on its inside bend, a place where egrets plod when the tide is in. On that day of talking to the crabbers, I felt I had left just before being overwhelmed by the urge to dash across the grass, leap into the low tide stream, and plod toward shore, doing some collecting myself. In the end I settled for poking among the slippery blades of rockweed, the presence of which indicated salt water, a note from the ocean just over the horizon.

I could not risk losing out on the next leg of my trip, wildways hunting northward up the other lanes of the Garden State Parkway, so I immediately swung north.

At 0.5 through 0.7 I was paralleled to the east by a wide flat stream and meadows.

At 2.3 to 2.5 I met another eastside stream, with its continuing meadow.

From about 3.1 to 3.4 lay the same pond you can see coming south at about this area.

Exit 3 takes you to Route 109 and, should you wish, Route 9.

5.1 to 5.3 offers you a long overlook from a high bridge. A stream with phragmites touches the Parkway at 6.3.

Exit 10 at 10.0 gives you Route 657 and the numerous places to visit that I have mentioned on the southward journey.

Eastward at marker 10.8 you meet the sea, but distantly over a broad flatland of salt meadow hay.

At 12.3 the green fuzz of catbriar makes you wonder of the possible uses of these climbing stems. Some people have found the new sprouts of spring and early summer edible. Roots of related species of Mexico, Honduras, and Jamaica have been used to give sarsaparilla.

At 12.8–12.9 and 13.4–13.6 you view wide expanses of salt marshes.

At 14.8–15.0, 15.8, and 16.0–16.2 you ride past drier meadows.

At 17.2–17.3 channeling divides the grasslands that lead to the ocean view.

You can pull into the Ocean View Service Area at 18.0.

You pay up at the toll booth of 19.5.

At 20.1 you can exit for Routes 9 and 50.

A long, broad channeled marsh sweeps toward the ocean between markers 20.7 and 20.9., with more marsh evident at 21.1, the broken view ending just before the picnic area at 22.6.

Perhaps while up on the bridge after 23.0, you think of how this gigantic prairie-like moment of land meeting sea, which continues through 23.6, would look near dawn or sunset. You hope to come here sometime when brightly white shore and sea birds are in their lanes, preferably those nearby.

You coast, as it were, onto salt marshes of 24.0–24. 1 and 24.4–24.5.

You can exit for Marmora at 25.0.

At 27.4 you know the massive meeting of fresh and salt water, in Great Egg Harbor Bay. Terrific shifts in salinity here are a constant challenge: fresh water forms risk losing body fluids, salt water ones fight the tendency of fresh water to invade their tissues.

One noon late in February scores of birds were at 28.1 swimming just off the northern sandy beach of the bay.

You can exit for Route 9 at 29.0.

Four tenths of a mile later you can see to your left how the salt wetlands reach west.

Patcong Creek is entering the ocean at 30.9–31.1.

At 34.7–37.8 see if the pines to your right don't have a very fresh-seeming tone.

265

At 36.9 you can take Exit 38 for Atlantic City, and just beyond at 37.3 the Atlantic City Expressway for Philadelphia and Camden.

Once again, at 39.1, you enter a pine-oak forest, so typical of the coastal plain and parts of the New Jersey Pine Barrens.

A stream gliding underneath the GSP at 39.3 is revealed by its black glinting water to the east.

Railroad tracks at underneath the GSP at 39.9 can prove to be rights of way to plants and animals from far places. Such refuges have since our western expansion led to movements of organisms both east and west, including an occasional tallgrass prairie plant that ends up among eastern railroad ties.

A service area turns up at 41.4.

Mountain laurel shrubs begin filling the wooded understory at about 42.1. They will blossom pink-and-whitely during spring; I have seen them form a high sash in the Great Smoky Mountains toward the first of May.

Poet Robert Frost would have enjoyed the retaining of leaves by the small white oaks along about 44.5. Young ones tend to keep their foliage all through the winter, and Frost wrote of the leaves that would slide out over the snow.

Here and there you may already have noticed the bundled leaves you can see at 48.1 up in the canopy, the winter nests of squirrels.

At 48.5 you swing up a bridge over the Mullica River and Great Bay and come down onto a great salt meadow.

At least one marina, viewed from 51.8, tells you of the river/ocean traffic operating around here.

An elegant marsh land spreads out and away to your left, westward, at 51.9.

The New Gretna Toll Plaza waits for you at 53.6.

You can enter other of the interesting parts of New Jersey at exit 58 (marker 58.4) by going off on Route 539 there.

Along about 59.8 notice how the pine branches swing out toward you, ever seeking light; the backs of the trees are essentially limbless.

The #63 exits put you off via Route 72 toward Manahawkin/Long Beach Island to the east and Camden/Chatsworth/Lebanon State Forest to the west.

During spring here on many years gypsy moth caterpillars have denuded oaks, especially such clusters of white oaks as you can note around 66.4.

At 68.9 you meet the Barnegat Toll Plaza.

At 70.2 exit 69 puts you on Route 532 toward Waretown and Forked River.

On this day I drove past a long forest of burnt trees, beginning about 71.3 and continuing for us to about 73.6. Such massive burns can help open the cones of pitch pine and powder the ground cover beneficially, destroying enough leaf cover so that the tiny seeds of pines could sink their roots into soil; this is so significant in the Pine Barrens that state-controlled burning has been done there to maintain the pineland as such, just as it was formerly done by the natural conflagration commonly caused by lightning.

A small creek winds under the GSP at 71.9. At 73.0 notice another but almost compelling wide-bellied black stream.

76.0 brings you the Forked River Service Area.

Exit 81 takes you to Lakehurst Road and Toms River.

At 80.4 you go over a slender stream through pines.

Exit 82 offers Route 37, to East Seaside Heights, Island Beach State Park, and West Lakehurst.

Exit 84 brings you Route 9 to Pleasant Plains and Lakewood

The Toms River Toll Plaza appears at 84.8.

Ninety-one miles up the GSP from its southern beginning, you find Exit 90, Route 549 to Brick Township and Point Pleasant.

Along about 94.1 the mowed lawns to right and left may remind you of some of the amount of care given to this, the Garden State Parkway.

Also as the mile markers here change, you may have noticed, as I was once asked to by a fellow passenger and observer of the nature here, the increasing hilliness, so typical of leaving the flatness but pleasure of South Jersey.

Exit 98 brings us full circle, if you have driven south with us, as we meet Routes 138, 34, and 195, the latter to take us again west.

THANKS TO

New Jersey Department of Environmental Protection, *New Jersey Outdoors*, "Not So Barren a Path"

The Wilderness Society, *The Living Wilderness* (now titled *Wilderness*), "Suspension" (poem)

Index of Places